CONTENTS

Nathan Coppedge

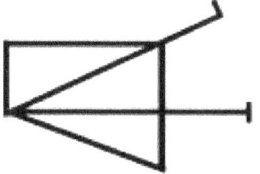

DIMENSIONAL
ENCYCLOPEDIA
VOL. II

Nathan Coppedge

Notation:

Psychology must remain open to new ideas. Indeed, if it were not for innovations in the set of concepts used by psychologists, the tradition would run adrift from the temporal zeitgeist. Much in the way of old-fashioned newspapers, it would no longer represent the feelings and motivations of the present-day. In writing this book I have made a significant effort to reach for new ideas, in fact, even a new method. However, because professional practice and public opinion leans heavily on traditions, my style has been one of modified imitation. I hope the reader will excuse the mixture of old and new ideas, as this has often been a characteristic of successful psychology.

Nathan Coppedge

THE DIMENSIONAL PSYCHOLOGIST'S TOOLKIT

or, The So-Called Serious Joke Book

By Nathan Coppedge

Nathan Coppedge

DEDICATION

This book is dedicated
honorably to the analytic
tradition, which advo-
cates that the dreams of
the self do not speak
against the soul of
the person. Amen.

Nathan Coppedge

INTRODUCTION

====================================

I make the important distinction that this is not a "People's" or "Capitalist's" book---not a 'social' book or a 'professional manual', in the full psychological sense in which these two principles may originally have been intended; Instead, the work spans a kind of intermediate territory, which I would like to make out consists still of psychology; yet, it may be said, this intermediate territory might be still considered radical; I am writing this book out of my obligation as a potentially eminent typologist; Consequently, the contents may be treated more like an experiment than as a diary of personal experience with patients and treatment;

The agenda of the Dimensional Psychologist's Toolkit is to provide an original standpoint on conventional principles; But it does this by considering what may be called a conventional context; Dimensionism as I define it *qua genus* might be considered more closely affiliated with art and philosophy, but the consequence of this is that it is a radical and consequently useful theory in the context of mental strata and human development; Initially and ostensibly the notion is to apply numbers to psychology; But I realize that endeavor may appear simplistic; So my efforts take root in many actual and clinical experiences of psychology's agons, with the hope that that empirical and contextual data-point is useful for what may be considered a general theory and mode for development;

Here we go a-Maying in the great field that is dimensional psychology; Who could deny the influence of mathematical and philosophical concepts in a field that has become more and more technicalized, and more and more dependent on artificial answers?; More often than not, there is a willingness to believe that the common traits of paradigmatic individuals or disease traits are results of generalitic social pre-determinations, or otherwise 'exceptionalist' traits that stem from very specific responses to environment; While I am not denying there is truth in this, there has been an uncommon willingness to pursue the intermediate territory between individual and social determination, and also to render objectively the facets of individualism and society of which these said pre-determinations consist;

The return to earlier categories in psychological thought is a return to an 'un-individualized' paradigm, a perspective that takes a broader view of the assumption that brains and situations are purely functionalistic; In this view, there is a necessary re-definition of religious and normative ideas; Afterall, these may not be innately understood, and if they are, it is possible that understanding itself poses some difficulty that is similar to neurosis or non-perspective; So, as a first tenet, I would like to presume separate the two magisteria (categories) which are most prevalent in psychology, namely pleasure and understanding;

If it is understood that psychology is still a young discipline, it is bearing on the entire 'map' of potential personal realities that there is learning which is yet possible, and some prior determinations may be ultimately as irreverent to the process of human thought and behavior as for example an entirely unrelated field, or even a happenstantial comment by a friend;

The first step towards dimensional psychology is what some might term 'quantification', however, realizing that this carries a degree of negativity along with excessive use, the prevalence that I speak of is more accurately a 'categorization' incorporating a degree of exclusivity; I have described this previously in my book, The Dimensional Philosopher's Toolkit, but here I mean to make its meaning adequate for the field of psychology;

If there is a tradition that has succeeded to categorize the soul without some degree of assumption (such as religiously, or by failing to grasp variety substantially) or a

13

concept of disease, I suspect that it has remained a cloistered or hermetic discipline which is not fully available to the common student, or predominately, for those whose sincerity in the pursuit of such study is at its freshest pique; So, frustratingly, in this endeavor to capture the entire field of psychology from a dimensional point of view, I have been forced to rely on my own opinions and respective critiques of pre-existing points of view; If there is a benefit in this perspective it is my angle as a philosopher, and the aforementioned view that perhaps most work in this field has been on the subject of disease, and is not therefore as theoretically grounded as some would assume;

In my viewpoint as a student of philosophy, it is necessary I find to alienate myself from the scientific opinions and even experiences of those who find themselves rooted in the field of psychology; I have observed a certain degree of sadism on the part of psychiatrists and even doctors, whose experience inevitably deals with manipulative personalities, different forms of negativity, and other so-called 'laboratory conditions'; Philosophy, as it differs from medicine, has a form of conservatism on the subject of human disease and paradigmatics that doctors may consider insipid or even stupid, but which may in some contexts of study, reveal the very strengths of the human mind which func-

tional medicine could not precisely comprehend, or at least, communicate; Psychology may benefit from the abstract perspective on qualities offered by sheerly abstract thought and communication, which
in some sense may be determined to be a
privilege beyond the scope of the pre-
determination that 'thoughts' and 'feelings'
are behaviorist, at least when we have not
determined that nature of psyche's 'desert
island';

Some would say that nature is determined
exclusively by sex, but I find in my loyalty
to philosophy a strange uneasiness with
any assumption that the origins of human
thought and action are not multifarious and
complex; For me, the complex vantage
point necessitates a view that is not primarily genetic, behavioral, or indeed hor-
monal; Instead, lives are functions of
'truths' which may be in many cases un-
stated, unchanged, or subtle by comparison to the judgments used about them; If
there is a remaining 'obvious' category
about the nature of the truths which affect
the psyche, it is in the correspondence and
coherence of the variety of truths, and the
dynamic, perhaps systematic ways in
which the truths express themselves; In
this sense, I am an 'Expressivist', and determine that whatever motivation 'ekes' out
of nature, whether it is of divine or historical, primitive or factual formulation, it is the
nature of this expression which determines
psychology;

15

Consequently, I find an inevitable truth that psychology is vastly dependent on circumstance, and when personal psychology is problematic and unresolved it is often because the context is unchanging and inflexible; There is thus a 'prior contingency' between thought and experience, with the effect that any function, however obscure, when it is adequate, is therefore entirely determinative for individual psychology; Individuals are only dysfunctional within their range of assumed responsibilities; So either one must determine that an individual is ignorant (which cannot be absolute, it seems), or there is a failure of priority, or finally a failure of world-function; While I am mostly consoled to the idea that most problems are faults of priority---that is, if we assume all problems are solvable, or otherwise preventable---there is an interesting stipulation in the idea that there is a kind of 'Pavlovian world' which treats functional beings as non-reactive; In this final case, which ignores 'blind problems' of the sheerly ignorant, it may be that the innate typological relevancy of some functional patterns have not been integrated with the functionality of social patterning; So, from one angle, it seems that individuals are 'behooved' to be social patterns, or else it has been determined for experience that experiences are not the point of departure for treatment; Otherwise we must assume that treatment is not the nature of the paradigmatic identity; And, obviously enough, it is not for us to think that functionality is impossible with no guarantee of treatment; Perhaps I have fallen into a consumerist mentality, but if that is the case, some others by contrast may have become legitimate 'zombie influences' upon the perspective of the consumerist youth;

It is this difference amongst zombies, consumer function, paradigmatic treatment, and individuals-as-social-patterns that runs through this book, a theme that I think is highly relevant to the most serious norms and conditions of psychology today; Perhaps functionalism has no choice but to create functional zombies, but what does this implicate about the rational legitimacy of a mental illness?; Can we afford to reduce mental function to an economic variable?; Aren't there 'sublime truths' which do not defer to pleasure?; One of my resulting theses is that there is a division, perhaps a schizophrenia, between 'simplified society' and the rational determination of the property of existence; Evidently one solution is materialism; But, as many people know, materialism itself may connote ignorance or even passivity--- which in turn affects the quality of functions; So that brings the argument full circle; Evidently it is argued that functional individuals are 'corporations'; But does this mean that individuals should function like corporations linguistically?; Formerly, psychologists expect the 'contingency to contingency' to be some sort of reassuring functionality; But of what does this functionality consist if the individual must be a corporation to hold up coherent language, or a 'authentic materialist' to find functionality?;

These and other questions are approached within the encyclopedic entries of this book, in an effort to resolve the local, yet ultimate question of the contemporary psyche, and its prevalence amongst the problems-provided;

Real inquiry into the nature of dimensional psychology begins with certain meaningful questions such as 'what are the affective aspects of psychology as it is reflected back upon the therapist?' and 'what dimension of disease cannot be reduced from function?'; Answering these questions is no easy task, and requires a degree of theoretical concern that may otherwise seem extraneous to analysis; The figure-ground of therapeutic process must originate with some specific comparisons and conceptual schemes which do not discriminate a great deal about the context of analysis; For example, enumerative concepts may be compared to the duality between functionality and madness to determine that, given complexity, only certain patterns are viable---if there are patterns at all; A logic tree can be formed in which it is concluded that either there is no logic, or functionality is not neutral, or madness in some cases is prospectively an enviable position; Dimensionism, which might otherwise be called superficial, ekes after certain neglected truths which by terms of a definitional sense of contexts, may seem serviceable;

After determining that function is the majority or minority, or that madness consists of certain exceptions to functionality which are common amongst many---even functional---types of cohort, it then behooves the psychologist to define a relative function in which madness or functionality has some proportional relationship within the context of re-assessment and evaluation;

If a given diagnosis does not relate with madness, there is a prospective for comparison, to the extent to which madness provides an accurate counterpoint or significant remainder upon the context of functional behavior and development.

============**PREFACE**=============

This book adopts an approach which considers multiple generalistic angles on psychological subjects; One of these is pretext, another is sur-text, and another is
post-text; Let me explain this method, one
I believe to be less arbitrary than average,
in its applications;

Two examples of *Pretext* are what might
be called the pre-conscious and the pre-
conscience; A number of things may be
said about them: (1) They exist in a continuum of development which may conceiva-
bly be stretched forwards or backwards,
(2) They express early examples of later
branches, in which later examples may
easily be imitations of earlier ones, thus
they are not unique, (3) At this point the
psychological role of the pre-
consciousness and pre-conscience within
the unconscious is reduced to a potential
absurdity: the primitive unconscious still
exists as a description of something which
may not have a name: it is both less predictable and more teachable than is commonly assumed; some of what is pre-
sumed to be the unconscious is merely a
formality concocted by serial non-
creativity, (4) Dimensionally, it is possible
that pre-conscious and pre-conscience are

not located ideas; Therefore, there is no
guarantee that these concepts existed in
their supposed locations, and there is no
guarantee that they are conditions to
which we will not return (they may exist in
the future rather than the past), Thus ends
a historical concept of psychology; (5)
Thus, fundamentally it must be accepted
that pre-conscious and pre-conscience
may be *values*, in the broad context, although not in specific problematic configu-
rations, (6) The conclusion then is that pretext is not to be seen developmentally, by
terms of a physical environment, but instead, known possible, by terms of a conceptual environment which 'inflects' development as a variable; Implicit in this is the
notion that one or another concept may at
one time have great bearing, while at another, almost none; The exceptions to this
are major ones, but often may be dis-
missed as idealizations: highly systema-
tized thought-as-object, coherent fantasies
which replace logic, and psychic integration with information, which provides superior reasons; That these three concepts
are sometimes interchangeable is a thesis
in itself;

Sur-Text is, at first glimpse, is a highly
contingent phenomenon; A psychologist
who embraces religion would be dumb-
founded to find that for some people, a
god is not the implicit mode of reference;
In a therapy setting, both the therapist and
the patient have a potential to debase

21

eachother's frame of reference; If we say that a psychologist has inevitably embraced some larger meaning or assumption, then sur-text is the concept that bridges the gap; (1) Initially, sur-text looks like pre-text: much concerns unconscious motivation, and unconscious influences; These are real elements, which exist partly because the therapist has embraced that the experience *is* a pretext; It is possible to move beyond this, and declare that the experience is a function of something that can be called sur-text; (2) Sur-text is revealed by analyzing the patient's *genuine* motivations; The patient is either confused, or has objects without meaning, or has meaningful objects, or has a whole sense of meaning; Any of these exist in degrees of truth, and under complex conditions of trickery; (3) Ask: is the patient finding an object? Then, is the patient finding meaning? Finally, is the patient confused? (These sort the person into the four categories of meaning listed above); (4) Is the patient getting what they want? If so, are they compatible with the type of meaning they are finding in life? Is it a case of weakness? Then respond to this; Is it a case of folly? Then respond to this; (5) The sur-text is the system of meaning which accepts the formal, conditional, and material aspects of the compatibility between desires and meaningful system (4 and 3); If the individual finds no meaning yet has a meaningful system, then he or she can be asked formal questions (Do you think your life is significant?, Do you think you are doing what you want to do?); If the individual has desire but the system is failing, then he or she can be asked about life-conditions which inform significance (Do you like your family? Do you enjoy the food that you eat?); If the individual suspends the question of confusion, he or she can be asked questions about reality in general (What is most real to you? How are you defining your life?); (6) Finally, sur-text is the general identification with meaning which may guide therapy; Whether it is pragmatic, or personal, or constructive, it is the formal element that must be understood or ignored; By referring to the sur-text, psychological problems become inflections which can be dealt with rationally, propensively the road to health;

Post-Text is the assessment of what happens as a result of a development; However, it is pre-figured by concepts of meaning from the sur-text; (1) Free-association raises a critical example of post-text: if another word or world can be imagined, then so to it must have some reality; Thus, what emerges otherwise is a conviction; This creates an implicit opposition between loyalty and imagination, suggesting that in some cases imagination is an exercise in fear; However, loyalty may be an exercise in folly, when meanings, objects, and confusions are incompatible; (2) Post-text also assesses that (fortunately or unfortunately) 'something must occur'; Thus, it can be

23

assessed if meaning follows from meaning, or object from object, or confusion
from confusion; Thus, development entails
causal variables, any of which may be byproducts; Sur-text remains central,
whereas pretext is disposable; (3) A clear
corollary is the meaningful by-product, for
otherwise the result is only continuity or
disruption; The patient can be asked if
sometimes continuity or disruption can be
meaningful, and if so, what this brings to
mind; The result is often a correlation between desire and meaning, and integration
with the concept that meaning (complex
and often imperfect) is the only form of
causality; (4) In specific cases, if the patient is not warned about consequences,
the result will be confusion; When the patient is given only material terms, he or she
will express confusion or conviction in that
context of reality; By contrast, when the
patient is given meaningful terms, he or
she will respond by seeking a meaningful
result; Examples of meaning are values,
understanding, and love used as information; (5) Post-text can become a method of
interpretation when a link is established
between significance and free-association;
Not only can the therapist interpret meaningful objects as functions of objects and
meaning, but the patient may develop an
ability to find new significances within the
old; This ability is clearly beyond what
might be called pre-conscious and pre-
conscience, so long as the conversation is
meaningful to the patient; Thus it may be

concluded that in the most developed conversations, the client has a conviction (loyalty) to significance, reflecting objective knowledge, a whole significance reflecting a meaningful, sometimes exterior system, or a confused significance, reflecting an inadequate system such as a failure of objects or a sense of paradox; In this sense, psychology becomes objective rather than what some have called 'obstreperous' or 'semantic'; (6) Post-text is also an inflection upon significance, a way of antiquating beliefs and gaining vicarious wisdom; Therapists and patients can be postmodern by psychically anticipating the antics of the future; When the patient is given confidence that some of these futures are significant but undesirable, he or she gains clarity about the shape of life and the value of the path chosen; If this is existential, it may also be transcendental; Post-text becomes ultimately, the bridge to the lives that could not be lived; And, also, an aspect of realizing what therapists call the sur-text.

Nathan Coppedge

FORE-NOTE

This text has taken the following quotation as a jumping-off point for general inquiry:

The real problem seems to be our need for, or insistence on, the absolute---a general human problem that lies beyond psychology. Yet this, our "beyond psychology," does not mean a simple acceptance of the modern emphasis on other factors, such as economics, politics or technique, determining human behavior... It means more psychology rather than less, but of a different kind. It is an emphasis upon the dynamic forces governing life and human behavior, in a word, the irrational

---Otto Rank, *Beyond Psychology* (p. 23)

Nathan Coppedge

==

A Conversation:

"Psychologists aren't supposed to believe in Babel"
---A Therapist

"Babble, babble, babble drives the poets insane"
---A Prescribing Doctor

==

Nathan Coppedge

≈≈≈≈≈A Second Conversation:≈≈≈≈

Patient: "So what is your opinion on appearances---Do psychologists have a general idea of surfaces?"

Therapist: "There is none. They don't have an idea of surfaces"

Patient: "Then how could there be a theory of meaning?…"

Therapist: "How could you have a theory of surfaces?"

Patient: "I think surfaces can be meaningful"

Therapist: "Thank you, you're right"

Nathan Coppedge

==

Important Statements of Prior Psychology:

Phase 1: Freud

[1] The collective unconscious dominates the rationality of dreams, [2] Sometimes values corrupt values, just as the sex drive creates and destroys evil

Phase 2: Jung

[1] Love is the rational force in the sense that it recovers the good of the ego, [2] Inspiration is a monster "a blond monster" that corrupts the preservation instinct

Phase 3: Behaviorists

[1] Mental illness is an inability to process information, [2] Normal or abnormal, in either case it may be a response to the environment

Phase 4: Situationists

[1] Society is a form of nature, when nature is possible, [2] Even artificial situations need authentic standards

==

Nathan Coppedge

THE DIMENSIONAL

PSYCHOLOGIST'S

TOOLKIT

Nathan Coppedge

===============A===============

Adequacy -

- The Four Lessons of Adequacy - [An intuitive approach]

Many people---nearly anyone---encounters difficulties which are commonly attributed to a lack of perspective; With perspective, life's troubles should be material at worst, and trauma should be past-tense; Commonly, people who report an adequate perspective also encounter little difficulty in the face of all but the most difficult encounters; It is clear that perspective makes a difference in encountering stress, thinking clearly, and not over-thinking or under-thinking a situation; In some sense, perspective thought is a different kind of thought; We know perspective is possible, and it often seems close at hand; I find that people are usually coping with four problems: [1] sacrifice, [2] arbitration, [3] indulgence, and [4] recognition;

FOUR CRUXES OF ADEQUACY

| SACRIFICE |
| ARBITRATION |
| INDULGENCE |
| RECOGNITION |

Commonly, everyone already addresses these points, but their perspective may be inadequate about them; Some begin with recognition and gradually cannot arbitrate an indulgence; Some begin with sacrifice and gradually fail to indulge in recognition; Some arbitrate everything, without indulging or recognizing the life that is being lived; Although these situations may result in evil consequences, approaching the root cause may be easy; It is not that the approaches are completely wrong, but they frequently miscalculate; The correct approach does a minimal job at addressing each of the four categories; The result is an application which works as well for life in general as it does for specific thoughts; The functional life accepts that to solve such a problem, the problematic category must be viewed as if it were a solution; Thus, in this case, each of the problems is actually a solution also; The difference is perspective::

Adler, Alfred - In what seemed like a lucid conscious-as-opposed-to-unconscious approach to therapy, he separated from Freud's school; The result, however, was ultimately to be concerned with two concepts: the inferiority complex, and the superiority complex; These concepts seemed unresolvable, leading to a difficult form of therapy in which he did not expect the patient to recover::

Affirmative Confirmation - The primary psychological theory in explaining the objectivity of the things people say; It follows an argument: (1) What someone says is something she or he thinks is true; (2) When it is true, there is a correspondence between the person and what she or he is referring to, and (3) When the correspondence is true, it also refers to something real, unless what is spoken of is imaginary; So, unless we mean imaginary things or dishonesty is implicated, there is some correspondence between what someone says and what is really true; This form of representation implies that the major hurdle to comprehension is the degree of understanding, not any mere 'theory' or 'hypothesis' of what may be so::

Affirming Evidence - See related material under Non-Statements;

Amalgam, The (Psychological Concept) - The amalgam is the stage between the so-called unformatted self and the basic functional self which I call the Unitarian. The Amalgam has a number of interesting properties, for example its ability to use influences for personal advantage, and its willingness to rely on 'ulteriors' for personal meaning. This self is often materialistic, and feels most successful when it has achieved some strategy of the mind or body which yields an obvious result. Depending on the person, its goals may be intellectual and technical, physical and technical, physical and non-technical, or intellectual and non-technical, and its sense of self depends on these types of categories. It may be seen as the 'selfish self' or even the 'original self,' however, it does not have the profound sense of being influenced which occurs with the Disintegral, or the success of the Integrator. However, the Amalgam is the most creative aspect of any person. This helps to understand how creative individuals are often slightly dysfunctional: they must look deep within themselves, to that time when they were neither influenced nor scripted: their own most original sense of self::

40

Apercu (Psychological Concept) - It literally means 'smaller thing' or 'key example'; The tradition of the apercu is deep with connotations of a doorway or theory which would egress upon a new unconcealed sense of meaning; However, in psychology apercu is a mental figure, a figure that connotes the precise mental state which prefigures an individual's realization; An apercu may be simple or complex, but so long as the person's associations remain the same, so too the apercu may be generalized between realizations; A functioning apercu is commensurate with predicting one's own intelligence; When this is not the case, often it brings stress; Some would say that intelligence itself is the apercu, others that it embodies a set of assumptions; However, in my view apercu is more specific; It is more cognitive than mere assumptions, and less generic than intelligence; Nor is it merely adapted intelligence or a formalization of assumptions; Apercu is the psychological state necessary for basic processing irrelative to stress; It is also the specific functions (nameless as they often remain) that an individual identifies with---whether they are rational or not---which connote higher functioning; In the endeavors to understand apercu, it may be that there are hidden social functions of cognition; It may be that small things loom large; Whatever the theory, the apercu appears to be an aspect of the mind which anticipates stress, yet which is modulated to respond to the broadest foreseeable variations in stimulation; As such it is not just simple or complex, it is also universal and personal; To make a statement against the apercu is to question the variables with which one assesses its reality; See also the Improviso and Permiscu::

Argumentation - The specifically sophisticated or naïve construction of language or responsiveness which establishes in a given moment the many assumptions or preparations which pre-figure an individual's concept of reality; The primary context of intellect::

Arrested Development as a Function of "Four Ideas" -

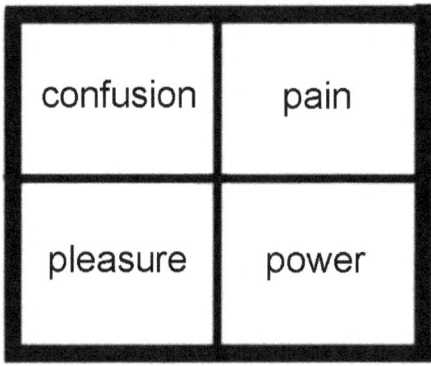

confusion	pain
pleasure	power

Stage 1: Here all progress is impeded by suffering.

The choice is to be tough.

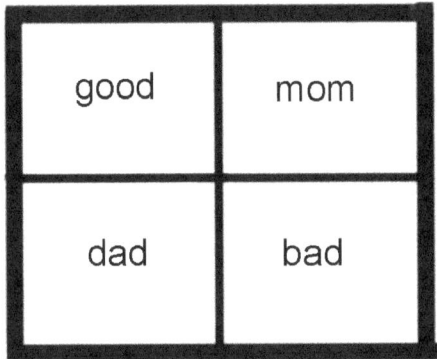

Stage 2: Here the parents are
conflicted about values.
The choice is to decide what's
right and wrong.

good neighbor	great family
crude enemy	appealing places

Stage 3: Here the child doesn't
emotionally grasp sexual abuse.
The choice is to confront fear

with wisdom.

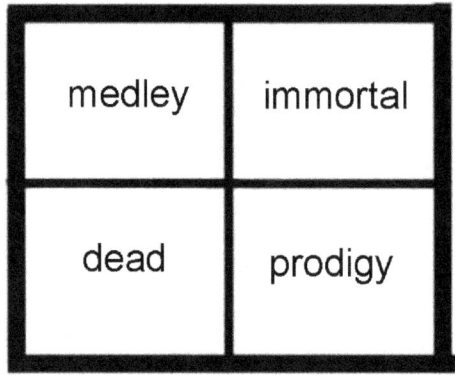

Stage 4: Here love seems to depend on people who are no longer alive.
The option is to abandon love.
::

Art Therapy - could easily have a systems component; Against the paradigm that patients make bad decisions is the paradigm in which patients are natural optimizers; Art therapy provides an opportunity to test the systems-level preferences of the individual; Afterall, it is the information age, a time of interactivity (and reciprocal research benefits); Dimensionism can be used as a basis for correspondences between forms of expression, which I believe to be the preferred art form of the mentally ill, following in the tradition of the popularity of the Rorschach test;

The problematic aesthetic of 'television

blotto' [multiplying depictions in a grid] is falsifiable, and can be transformed into perspectival, emotional-developmental, and especially thought-interactive forms::

Artistic Virtue - Few would say that artists are ill-intentioned; But what would make an artist virtuous? Surely its not something so crass as a material product; But we must posit that it is possible for an artist to have good intentions; Yet, afterall, it is not conveyed directly in any form; The artist is neither an actor nor an oblique conversationalist; So, what about art makes the artist virtuous when it is not the material product?; If the motive is complex, it may be misguided or even foolish; However, the innocence of the artist's intent provides a foundation; Say, that when an artist---or by extension, as is usual, anyone with the slightest artistic bent---has an innocent intention, then this is a significant blank slate ---arguably, however, it may be a platform gradually, through the environment, for some negative impulsivity, or not: what makes the difference? Evidently, the artist, to have virtue, must be a platform for his own innocence; Any genius, be it for form, or novelty, or mere preoccupation, sustains the artist's innocently intended and virtuous mode of operation; If there is a problem with this, it is only by suppressing or stimulating an incorrigible urge; Thus it provides a basis for intellectual guidance::

The insensitive conclusion with **Asper-ger's Syndrome** is that it is never as sim-ple as value; But a less complicated an-swer is that it always involves higher math; But to the individual, there must be some highly symbolic connection, which renders 'math' literally the subject of life; Another option is to abandon stereotypes, and at-tribute Asperger's to a variety of highly de-veloped intelligence-behaviors; It can be seen that social function in some cases depends on fixed types of relationships between curmudgeonly possession of knowledge and outward responsible ac-tions; Taking the naïve view, apparently (or un-apparently), value is the concept returned in this context of subjects, sug-gesting that Asperger's relates with some kind of constructive psychology, or at the worst, some form of self-induced repres-sion. Clearly a more responsible under-standing would be that the person with As-perger's seeks some kind of high-level as-sessment function, a transformative repli-cation of elements of 'ordinary' society and other truths, in which math or some other system becomes the profound lemma::

Aspiantialism - (Literally, 'hermeticism'); The ability to provide meaning to specific procedures such as entering a house or doing laundry; One theory has it that it cor-responds to full, ordinary function, another that experiences such as that of a millionaire 'use up' functions, another that the functions are infinite or constructive, and the most extreme theory finally is that psychopaths are creative with it; The correspondence amongst the theories promote necessary conflict, for example the millionaire may have specialized functions the psychopath doesn't have, and an infinite construct is not always a construct of ordinary functions; However, clearly the most prevalent theory is that aspiantialism concerns the development of routine, ordinary functions, and not creativity, for or against psychopaths; (See opposite at Itineralism)::

Attraction -

Conventional and Unconventional Attraction and Modification: Consider the case of a single father who is effeminate and has a son; The son, if he lives with his father, will seek someone who resembles his father; Society will then modify the behavior to seek someone who does not look like his father; Consider another case: the father is single, masculine and unattractive; The son lives with his father and seeks anyone who does not look like his father; Society then modifies his behavior to be 'more like his kind' and seek someone unattractive;

The case is different in more conventional cases, say, of a married couple; Either the child will deviate and seek the more attractive appearance of the two, ignoring gender, or the child will attach to the opposite gender, perhaps blindly; It is interesting that, if beauty is not associated inextricably with gender, the individual may disassociate sexuality from sex, developing a kind of 'beauty fetish' that has been associated with Narcissus; The opposite occurs in purely functional relationships where sex is seen as a kind of unthinking coincidence; For reasons like these, intellectualism has been a kind of opponent to functional relationships, a kind of obsessive detractor, which does not always even get fetishes right; Yet, ironically, intellect is often granted considerable authority, perhaps for the benefit of a theoretical advantage-seeking minority; Theories of energy dominate media, while passive conservation dominates real actions; If there is an exception to this, surely it is in manifest evidence, for people are often looking for deviations to compare with themselves, however couched they happen to be in notions of 'normalcy' ::

Aubadism (awb-A-dizm) - A term borrowed from poetry that applies to some special cases; Specifically, a certain impulsiveness which develops in the morning --- The poetic term refers to lovers parting at dawn; Women in particular may have a trend of repressed evil feelings that mounts at this time, and this is likely the prime psychological source of difficulty, while the male counterpart may be more aggressive, but is sometimes marked by uncertainty; The healthy response is to use this energy for life planning, as sometimes is the wont of those pre-disposed for early experiences in intimacy; At least, this explains some of the emotional payoff concurrently; Essentially, it is a deciding factor for risk and reward and it may be noted that the results of this daily conflict---if it occurs---may go unobserved by the psychologist::

Aversion [topical studies]- tends to be associated with some outer characteristic, just as people are more likely to dislike others than to dislike themselves; This is especially proven when it is realized how little response is often merited to others' specific concerns; Indeed, the loathing of other types of people is endemic, (partly a function of a complex lack of inspiration) but it is also suppressed; For example, at times in history outward actions of some nations have been limited to military conflict and economic grappling; The genuine empathic element is traditionally the family; Indeed, alienation outside the family has been a key reason to reinforce social ties in the West; However, the view that the exterior is the point of criticism raises the concern that the modality is superficial; For a contrary view, we need look no further than the philosopher Plato, who said that ugliness is a form of character associated with manliness and courage; While clearly this *modae* seems slightly outdated, civilization has done little to replace it; Instead of finding a new desirable ugliness to the soul, people have obsessed over the perpetuation of exterior means and agencies, which essentially amount to superficial psychology; Clearly aversion of the true form requires an identification with the 'exterior self' which can then be treated as soulful *or* beautiful::

===============B===============

Behavior as Affect - It has long been recognized that behaviorism is a form of functionism; The implication, however, is that behavior *is* a form of affect; Behavior, behavioristically, is a function of the person, the environment, the culture, the functional paradigm, and any other factors, all of which are affects that the person is trying to evoke; If not, there is not a form of behavior being expressed, or we can say that what is expressed is an empty function, that is either behavior or function, but not both; But, however, behaviors require functions, and it is clear that behavior in the source that is observed, is not every purely functional; Indeed, behavior is a surface; Behavior in general can be defined as a surface with a function (or more than one function); It is then only up to the imagination to determine that the surface may be dynamic, and the function may originate inside or outside the individual; When both interior and exterior are evoked, we do not determine that 'there is no surface', but rather that it is the surface being evoked; There is no denying that a surface can still have a function, but that is not to say that it is purely functional; And, denying that behavior has functions or surface could be ridiculous; Adding a third factor looks like a modification of definition, rather than the arrival of a new concept; In dimensional psychology, the use of behavior as a functional surface is useful for its compatibility with the existence of time and space, and how it provides a razor for determining the complexity of a personality; After this determination, confusing personalities are ersatz, but not necessarily crazy; Afterall, new concepts may be new functions, and affect is not itself rational, is it?::

The **Buzz of Ideas -**

THE BUZZ OF IDEAS

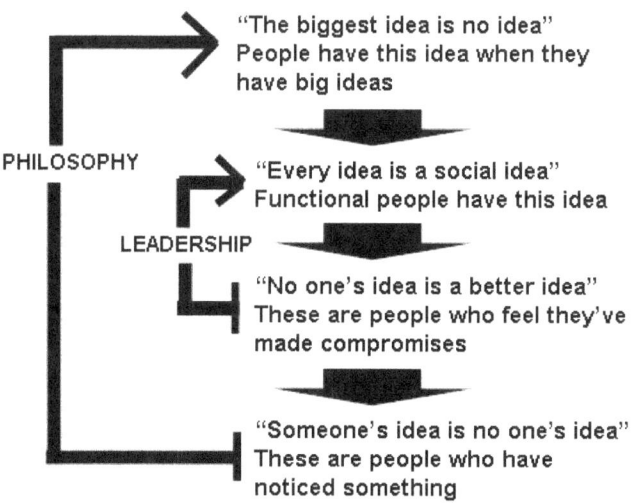

PHILOSOPHY

"The biggest idea is no idea"
People have this idea when they
have big ideas

"Every idea is a social idea"
Functional people have this idea

LEADERSHIP

"No one's idea is a better idea"
These are people who feel they've
made compromises

"Someone's idea is no one's idea"
These are people who have
noticed something

::

==============C===============

Case Studies (Using Deductive Methods) -

Micro People: Virtual reality environments may allow some to live miniature lives; My assessment of this is that micro people seem to experience much longer lives: the sense of time becomes inflated with the sense of frenetic activity, and how easy it is to accomplish the simplest tasks; What this suggests is a general rule in which to some extent the experience of time inflates when the body shrinks; While that may not be true between species and at extreme extents of age (or debilitation), it provides a promising and somewhat sensible clue to dimensional organization of biology qua-psychology at a fundamental level; (Similarly, giants may report that years pass like the movements of the foot when walking: while other lives seem less significant, they also seem to have more bearing on time; If it is time that is significant, then little people start to seem more significant);

Slumbering People: There is some evidence to show that sleep is the conservative state of the body; Therefore, the large cohort of people who sleep represent also the cohort of people enacting a conservative state of mind (here I think I am ignoring local usages); We also know that most people have dreams on a weekly basis, and that the body adjusts itself to bed partners; However, if sleepers are conserving the significance of dreams, they are also participating in what is called the collective unconscious, defined not as both a waking and sleeping state, but only as a sleeping one (that is, if it occurs while waking, this is because the mind is partially asleep, participating with the conservative trend); They are, in a sense, adjusting their bodies to other people whether or not they sleep with them; The alternatives are that they are uncomfortable or ignorant; So what could this sleeping conservatism consist of? Only communication (of some degree), brainstorming, serving purposes like alleviating boredom, and planning life; Most people already seem to know this; As an alternative, consider that the body adjusts itself selfishly or hermetically; Then how will we know if it adjusts itself to other people? Evidently it is inherent or meaningless, yet has psychological bearing;

Toy Landscape: Children and adults performing activities in a toy landscape displayed characteristics of power-wielding and egotism; These characteristics were more prevalent amongst adults than children, suggesting that the qualities were directly proportional to the size of the person's body; What is less reported is that the power-wielding is analogous to self-control and hence rational assertiveness; Ignoring the superficial unusual aspect of the toy landscape (which arguably reduces to its novelty), it seems that the smaller the landscape is---indeed the smaller any object is---the more it seems significant once proven meaningful; The direct analogy is (1) The Alphabet, which may set a nominal standard of significant scale, and (2) Human semen, which has the implication of constructing life; Even aside from the sexual, theological, or nihilistic implications of this, there is a potential for a paradigm shift towards larger, more emotional significances; Perhaps determinism especially, is contingent on the simpler rather than the larger; But according to a toy landscape, it is relative; Correspondence is required; Large ideas must be plural, whereas singular ideas must be danglers::

Categoresis - The way people tend to functionally exhibit categories; These categories may be of certain types, for example 'approximation of merit', 'legal sawyer', and 'color me married'; Interestingly, the categories may have highly personal meanings, which are as potentially adaptive as they are nevertheless a function of highly specific memes; If the memes are ultimately the zone of creative enterprise for these people categories, it seems unfair, but it provides a common ground of parlance; What emerges is: (1) A search for definition, (2) A theoretical landscape, (3) A system of social affirmations or denials, and (4) A sense of reciprocity (See Adequacy); It is not surprising that in this age of information what is required is information reciprocity, just as at another time the context would be bonhumor, chivalry, or 'nerve'; In any case, the expression of the category is often indirect and outwardly deniable, but carries a grain of truth to the inner personality (and there are variations on this in which the entire expression is superficial, raising questions of the meanings of the obvious)---say, for intellectual, social, or even secret reasons; Thus my thesis of intrigue in psychiatry is that it concerns secret categories of personality---essentially the choice is between a coherent, common language, where everything is free, and a secret, hidden language that can dote on its own privileges; Both have dimension, but one embodies knowledge, while the other embodies mastery; The dynamic of categories is forever rejecting its knowledge for some new temporary principle; This text has provided an intuitive and generic guide to what I call categoresis; (In philosophy the meaning is slightly different, and refers to dynamic categorical methods)::

Channeling Objectivity - has an obvious role in clarifying factual instances so that rational decisions can be made; Partly this role is already played by families, hospitals, and perhaps sometimes even the media; But where the media is said to be biased towards consumerism, the family is said to be biased towards a variety of factors, such as image ('appearances'),

pleasure, or impulsivity, in a sense structuring beliefs in a way that may not be objective; In hospitals, there is an assumption of weakness that can be heavy-
handed; Under the assumption of weakness it may be difficult to be objective
about self-worth; So when we talk about
channeling objectivity, we generally refer
to personal techniques or psychology
proper to determine its significance; The
less obvious role of objectivity is delineative, and is structured according to rules as
to whether boundaries may be crossed; In
one sense, the areas defined by the
boundaries may be useless, but this is
only the case where there is not meaningful delineation; One clear expression of the
delineative function is to intermediate between inner and outer self; (It can also be
used to produce insights about other topics of interest); The outer self is the self
concerned with other people, ambition, in-
dulgences, etc. The inner self is the pri-
vately cultured self, the nurturing of which
brings happiness; It may be innocent, or
wise, or foolish, but the objectivity of the
outer world will involve crossing the
boundary and addressing both how one
feels and how others perceive the self;
This is extended still further when key insights are needed about a client's life and
volition, in which case one may do well to
find key examples of the hidden aspect
which may then be used as positive and
negative influences---abstract conditions to
avoid or affirm in life::

Circumstantial Knowledge –

CONDENSED BUT REFUTABLE TRUTH:
SKELETON TREE AND
1-DIMENSIONAL VIEWS OF MEANING

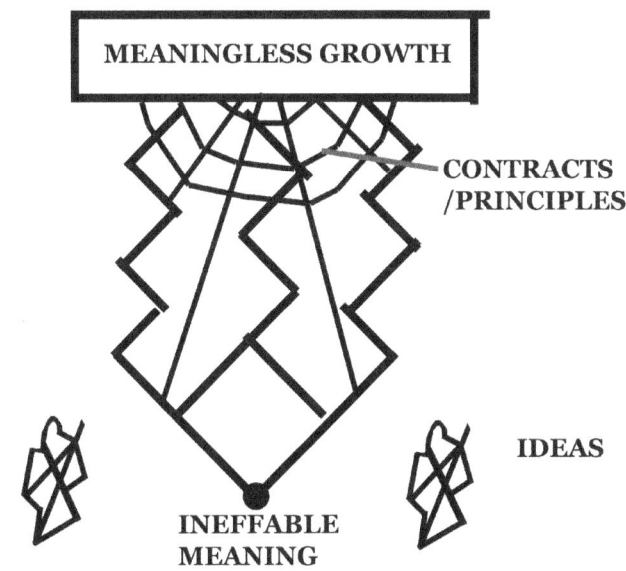

MEANINGLESS GROWTH

CONTRACTS
/PRINCIPLES

IDEAS

INEFFABLE
MEANING

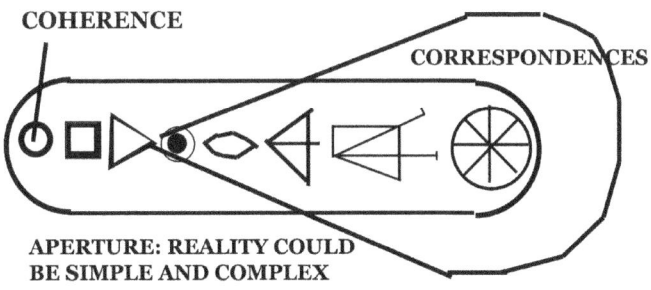

COHERENCE

CORRESPONDENCES

APERTURE: REALITY COULD
BE SIMPLE AND COMPLEX

::

Clinical Studies - When children think of a clinical setting, they think of a whole cloud of potentialities. And by and large, this is made all the more complex by the hazy relationship between thinkers and doers--- something like comparing flea studies to Schrodinger's Cat. Reports occasionally surface of a patient who is as sanguine as a child. That the reasoning of a subject could be as coherent as a laboratory report. These are often had in statements such as "I'm not hungry, it means I need to sleep," or "I'm not on antidepressants. It means I'm not depressed." Such cases seem to illustrate a certain negative resolution to the interviewing process and clinicalism in general, either by the unconscious urge of the individual, or some innate wisdom contradicted by artificial countenances. Little attention has been paid to the role psychology plays in the emergence of these "thoughts." Such elements can be seen interplaying with broader notions such as sociology, *geographie* , and impulsivity. Such elements as a patient's own insular understanding should be appreciated for their quality, not their dissolutedness::

Close Logic of Well-Doing - Close logic in this case is an expression of the theoretical ability to condense perceptions if they meet a certain standard, a standard of morality, in this case the standard of doing good acts; Not only could good acts simplify a life, but they provide a standard or example for achieving control; It can be argued that other types of achievements would also simplify a life, but nonetheless it remains true that good acts simplify a life; By choosing 'good' and choosing 'acts' the choice is one for meeting a basic standard 'good' (interpreted pragmatically or otherwise), and the imperative to act, in order to prove that something is accomplished at all; The two go hand in hand, is another reason why this particular choice is the condensation of the broader case; While placing restrictions on achievement might mitigate the effects, such as under totalistic demands, with a relative standard of the presence of values, some value may provide some assertiveness, just as some assertiveness potentially creates values; That double-character of values and assertiveness characterizes the close logic approach, as one in which subtle freedoms are granted by allocations of commitment; With some exploration and a capacity to negotiate for opportunity, there is a potentially vast expansion of those same subtle freedoms::

Collective Unconscious -Sources have differentiated the collective unconscious from the ordinary concept of an unconscious mind;

Antic View of the Unconscious:

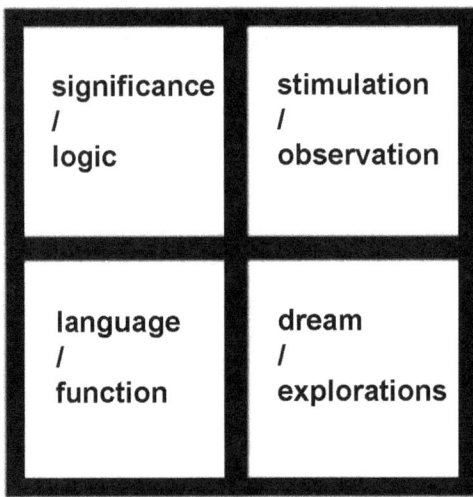

significance / logic

stimulation / observation

language / function

dream / explorations

(Continued on following page)

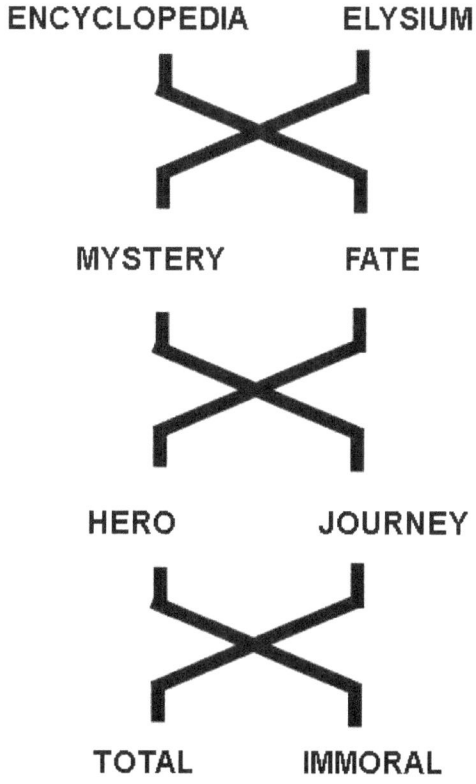

ENCYCLOPEDIA ELYSIUM

MYSTERY FATE

HERO JOURNEY

TOTAL IMMORAL

(Continued on following page)

"Golden Braid of the Unconscious":
Notes on the Braid:
(1) Dreams of heroes and dreams of language,
(2) Logic is a mystery or fate because it is a stimulation; The meaning it has relies on language (concrete functions) for certainty; By that time it is looking for a dream;
(3) The hero is not a journey: they are symbols of language;
(4) The only moral choice is to embrace totality, because the incomplete person, it is said, cannot gain except selfishly; The total person adequates greed or humility, depending on which reflects the true character of the person::

Comic Sans - A traditional view would hold that seriousness is a product of pragmatic interest; The lives of those committed to ordinary, purposeful work; In this context, it is sometimes said that it is only the fool who questions this behavior; Certainly, however, some pragmatic lives will admit of humor; The danger, obviously enough, is that humor may be unbalancing to the tradition of normalcy; Humor cannot always be classified as normal, and approaching the question of 'what is normal about humor?' raises doubts about the general classification of normalcy; For example, a question may be raised as to whether someone with a small defect is normal, if the defect is obvious, versus someone with a hidden problem that turns out to be quite serious; Although these are normal questions, they do not always have standard answers; For example, if the serious ailment is curable, whereas the small problem is incurable, one may be tempted to believe that any curable problem can recover normalcy; But at that point, such problems begin to define what it means to be normal, in turn affecting the meaning of humor and dishumor, and also pleasure and displeasure; At least, the question then becomes, what is without humor, that may preserve the function of normalcy? Must normalcy be a charade?; Four categories emerge: (1) Labor against weakness, the case of doctors, (2) Labor with death, the case of soldiers and morticians, (3) Serious humor, such as the life of a clown or comedian when they take their job seriously, or professional humor, or (4) A battle against humor such as what children encounter at school; Clearly these options provide a variety of fixed choices when it comes to avoiding humor; Consequently, humorlessness is constantly marked by very fixed patterns of thinking and behavior; An irrationalist may question these areas saying, very few people work as morticians, no one should work as a soldier, children may be avoiding monstrosities in the process of growing up, and the doctor's dishumor does not add to his work; But where does this leave us?

Clearly dishumor is a response to problems; But this does not mean that the converse, humor, is any more natural; Apparently people thrive on neutrality, to which may be added any passable specialized behavior; The world thrives on actors, who must use humor or comic sans as a rhetorical position with a merely assumed degree of legitimacy; What makes actions passable is not humor or dishumor, but some other factor::

Conceptualism - has been a bane of psychology, since it attracts evasive personalities; However, it is a goal of dimensional psychology to unite psychology and conceptualism; A beginning point may be found in psychological products; Some of these are even aimed at students who may be mentally ill, leading to an interesting point that some degree of input in psychological products may come from the mentally ill; If not, one may choose to 'naturalize' the instituted formula so that it serves the special interests of higher functions; That is, if one assumes that mental functions do not ever correspond with mental illness specifically---as by inspiration, extremism, or a selective character of language; Perhaps, for example, madness is a valid archetype only for the mentally ill; Or perhaps mental health is always mapped in terms of a breadth of prior experiences---much like the Buddha's encounters with age, illness, and death; What emerges more often than not, is some set of category-symbols which must be called un-synthetic; From such a set one may determine modes of correspondence which affect the conscious symbols of psychology, not just for the practitioner, but also for those that would buy a psychological product; Perhaps where this is leading is an all-inclusive psychological game, leading to a broader range of intellectual influences;

Conceptualism and Childhood Development; It is important to realize the co-dependent relationship of kind affection and conceptual systems in childhood development; Genuine affection builds rationality at a fundamental level or orients the individual child to key hereditary-genetic attributes which in turn affect future development; Conceptual systems, whether they are symbolic, expressive, or free/arbitrary constructs, have the potential to reinforce trust and skill with long-term commitments when emotional reinforcement is available; If there is a material incentive in cognitive development, it is reinforced not through direct symbolic representation, but instead through fulfillment of adequacy; Through generalities, however effluent and robust, specific skill-sets are realized; The exception to this rule is largely a function of demands placed on the individual; Four parts of the development of conceptualization, mirroring intellectual development in a modular fashion, can be described in quadra:

67

Adequacy	Commit-ment
General-ity	Demand

::

Condescension seems to distinguish a type of personality which in some other cases is better related to a personal or religious charisma; However, condescension, determined from an individual's ugliest moments, serves as an index of the negative elements of arrogance; For example, when this condescension is suppressed or introverted, this may spell a relation to a specific mental health disorder, almost in a virtuous light, e.g. by understanding the motivations for the arrogance; Foundationally, arrogance in general is only ever justified by acting outwardly, such as intellectually, relationally, or violently; For some cases this arrogance is embodied by social class, while in other cases more problematically, by social affiliations or an often temporary personal agenda; Condescension can be traced out situationally to be a response to stress or a form of developed personality; The first form in repeated instances will often lead to the second; Given certain conditions, such as similar employment or conditioning, a son or daughter of an arrogant person will repeat aspects of the father's or mother's arrogance; However, in some cases called deferred arrogance, there will be only a superficial resemblance, and the condescension will 'lose its teeth'; Sometimes this is the case when the second person's childhood was not as demanding, whether or not there were professional pressures; Where condescension as a developed personality may often be of the deferred type or relate to social or religious views, condescension as a response to stress may have a different and yet interesting character; For it is observed sometimes that a person becomes more condescending in reponse to doting behavior ('spoiling'), particularly when the doting occurs without a traumatic event; This may even be enhanced when there is a notional trauma without traumatic effect, as in the case of losing teeth or surviving a conflict; Thus, most forms of condescension are formatted in a 'proving ground', confirmed by religious and social opinion, and left fundamentally unchanged from the initial context of reference; Therapy techniques might focus on the changeable personality, the cause of stress, and religious or social beliefs::

In most cases, medical care relies on **Consortium Answers,** for example corroborations between treatment and authority, informational and functional organization, or decisions based on individual agent versus consensus in the context of organization; On a second level, this form of functionism ties the individual to the organizational, and therefore to icons or symbols of function, including doctors, medicines, scientists, and business leaders; On yet another level of consortium, there is a potential logic for organization between actual experiences of these elements which need not be entirely opaque; To some extent this last function is served by the public and professional media, which increasingly depends on commercial stimulus for a motivation to corroborate the various sectors of functionism; As populations grow, there is a greater potential for corroboration, but agents of 'insight', 'stimulus', and 'hard answers' are at a premium; When the individual, social, and functional-bureaucratic levels are connected in a dimensional system, there is a strong dependence on this last degree of connection, and any degree beyond it; But, consortium answers look hollow if there is not an oblique pursuit of meaning, qualities, or in other words psychology in its most adequate form, which may be by terms universal, private, and functional, through realities which are either obvious or disregardable::

Consummate Information - goes a long way towards explaining the source of individual motivations; When motivations are not genuine, they always participate in a process of disambiguation; Either the moti-

vations become clear, or they remain ob-
fuscated; In either case the individual
loses some control; These personalities
become passive actors as long as they are
ingenuine; The genuine cause of action
may be attributed to someone more genuine, who if not absolutely in control of
those effects, at least participates responsibly in managing some sort of
'consequence' for his or her own life; But
because the chain of effects is not absolutely personal for anyone except selfishly
and thus inconsequentially, the genuine
source of action is also an impersonal at-
tribute; People share in 'resemblances' of
actions which may have effects whether
they are genuine or not; What this means
actually is that the individual must
'consummate' his or her actions by being
more or less genuine; But this action of
consummation is essentially impersonal; In
many cases it is as though someone else
made the decision, hence a reflection not
of individual authenticity, but some sort of
surrogate or forgery; Relatively speaking,
that this authenticity is false may be unim-
portant; For it is not necessarily the duty of
the individual to create the impersonal
source of authenticity; What is clear, however, is that the cause of motivation is im-
personally consummated by authenticity,
for the source cause of motivation is relatively genuine; See also Psychic Facts::

71

Contingerion - When only one aspect of life must be given vitality there is an effect of contingency; The single aspect comes to dominate the consideration for any quasi-vital category, producing a ripple effect; At some point, however, of adding vital categories, that paradigm is replaced; Instead of being affected by a single specific criterion (however complex), the criterion itself is contingent upon contingency itself or life itself; Thus there is a choice between property existence (singularity), contingent existence (struggle), and 'life itself' (the property of struggle); This last part may be difficult, even though quantifying and experiencing life seems tantamount to success; People may identify the best characteristics present during a move or relocation; That quality differs from the singular property that existed in the United States in the 1960's, where single influences dug into everything; Even if the effect was not unpleasant, the effect of the zeit, love, or peer pressure (as soft as it may have been, there are not always words for it), could still seem like an immovable wall; So the question of psychological contingency is really a question of three things: (1) The necessary importance of any one thing, (2)The quantification of things which may be vital, and (3) The ability to find properties of vitality within the categories; The result of combining the three is the contingerion: vitality scales to the authenticity and quantity of categories, when they are vital; Then it can be determined such questions as 'Do I like math' or 'Do I need time alone'?::

Conversation Conflict - Even with hearing voices aside, there is a conflict in the internal conversation of many people; This is the conflict between public opinion and self-assertiveness, between extroversion and introversion, and between noise and silence; I will abbreviate it as the relation between silence and noise, as there is a heavy-handed argument which says that we do not always know that we are original people; If we did, we might not be inspired by our own thoughts and beliefs; Not only is there a kind of unexpected disbelief and veil of ignorance on the subject of continuity, there is also an addictive dependence on narcissistic affirmations to justify the life -progress; This is all assuming the individual is not fully functional emotionally; In reality, there are some individuals who are entirely without these conflicts; However, a problem still remains for them: the problem of 'perfect' silence or 'perfect' noise; When these are abandoned, he or she is likely to discover his or her own humiliating superiority to other people; At that point, there is a need for a veil of understanding, something she or he may not yet even comprehend, in spite of everything; This stage is the emergence of the real ego, where it is common to mistake differences in reality for differences in truth::

===============D===============

Darwinian Circle - Two diagrams remonstrate a potential relationship between survival and delusion:

DARWINIAN CIRCLE AND PSYCHOLOGY

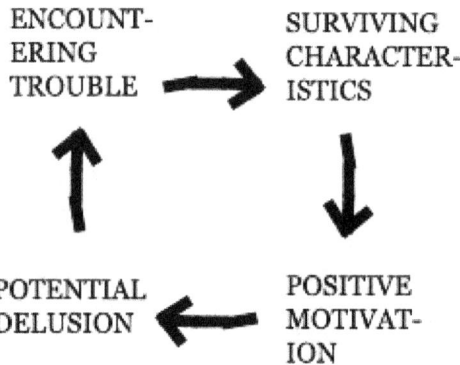

ENCOUNT-
ERING
TROUBLE

SURVIVING
CHARACTER-
ISTICS

POTENTIAL
DELUSION

POSITIVE
MOTIVAT-
ION

DARWINIAN CIRCLE 2

SO MUCH IS A PROBLEM

SO MUCH IS A SOLUTION

These do not demonstrate so much implacable values as product conditions, e.g. earlier and later stages will show less or more relationship amongst the displayed categories, respectively, showing a need for complex interpretation; Reducing a scenario to meaning, may for example be more effective than reducing the same scenario to motivation; This has implications for both paranoid and depressed types, in their respective responses::

Demon of Deduction - Unlike philosophy, where a given set of reasons can be embodied in an organized system, psychology relies upon the strength of the individual, a less objective answer; The demon of deduction follows from what some encounter as a futile process of self-definition; It may have a beginning point that is abstract or materialistic, such as 'aren't we material beings?' or 'I serve my senses' and devolving first when a specific value is imposed, decreasing the strength of the generalism, and secondly when it is determined that the specific value is bankrupt; Although it can be substituted with chemistry, people may find that chemicals are no inherent substitute for a strong set of reasons; While some merely disagree, others may find the demon of deduction insurmountable; Solutions in therapy may range from chemical stimulation, to instruction on nutrition or even rhetoric (See also the Sacrificial Dilemma)::

75

Despotic Mood - One of the major quasi-functional mood types, often seated in a conventionalizing or de-conventionalizing of common attitudes towards others' motivations; In the case of de-conventionalizing the response may be a reaction to outright conflict, or a reaction to a peculiar determination of self-motive, that is, out of a previously hidden guiding force; In the case of conventionalizing, it may be a response to general social forces, or a reaction to imputations of personal responsibility; These motivations explain how despotic natures have a potential to be dangerous, mostly because they are so personal, and may often connote---at least originally---some sense of guilt about responsibility (which may reasonably be conflated with a sense of authority or self-motivation); In the case of children, despotic nature may suggest naïvete about these same forces of concern, namely authority and personalization; When it is developed from an early stage in life, the so-called childish nature contends ownership of its problem, creating a confusion when others attempt to broker concern or decidability; With greater forceful motivation, the despotic nature can treat others like pawns in a game; But at the same time, it is playing a game with itself; Factors like resolution, knowledge, or emotion could force uneasy contentions to what begins as a personality, and often continually manifests in experience::

Diagnostics -

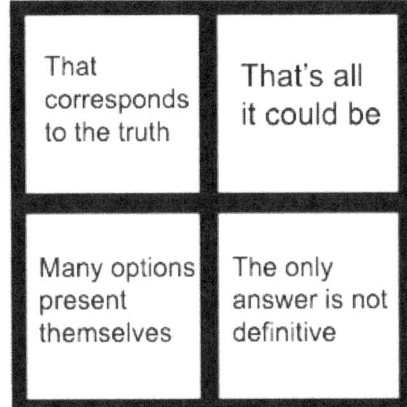

::
::

Dialectic of Functional Psychology - (1) The person should be concerned for the good things, often abstractions because life is not ideal. This prevents empty feelings. (2) Err on the side of caution. By this rule major psychological problems can be avoided. On the other hand, the person may appear dangerous if they express fear. This leads to repression. Back to the good things.

Dishonesty - Lying may be important in the context of psychotherapy; Dishonesty, of both simple and complex types falls into two categories: non-expressive and crea-

tive; Simple non-expressive lies have a
character of simple affirmation combined
with non-creativity; Simple creative lies
have a character of outright denial and a
consumer approach to hypotheses; If the
two types are combined, they have the
negative character of both types; Complex
dishonesty is just the abverse of the simple types: in the non-expressive type there
is a subtle negation combined with creative hypotheses, and in the creative type
there is repeated affirmation combined
with a thought-out method of manipulation;
More advanced forms exist, for example
seeking forms of satisfaction as a foundation for a confidence game; The more advanced forms are ubiquitous in politics,
typically even translated as forms of individual ethics, conduct, or belief; However,
these advanced traditional types do not
always have the localized negative effects
affiliated with typical lying; The effects are
more likely to be global, affecting different
types of conditions, such as economics,
business policy, or academic standards::

Disintegral, The (Psychological Concept)
- There is a reason why trauma occurs frequently during the earliest years of life.
This is a time when individual beings are
most sensitive physically, intellectually,
and emotionally. The greatest promise of
personal success comes from positive
early influences, and the worst promise
comes from negative influences during this

time. The Disintegral is the searching, primordial self: the self most willing to make sacrifices, and the self least-willing to accept failure. I call the Disintegral by this name, because, usually, no matter what happens, some aspect of this primordial self is lost---it disintegrates---. Rarely do we connect with the full vital potential we were once aware of in our very earliest years. We felt connected with God, or politics, or the most profound ideas. We were believers in magic and reincarnation. The self of that time is confronted with monumental facts which do not honestly explain themselves. Facts become twisted against the admission that everything is plain and ordinary. Later, there is a sense of guilt that something magical did not happen. Or perhaps it did, and it was part of the degeneration. In any case, the Disintegral is the most powerful aspect of the self, but it is also the most conflicted. It depends on others, and especially upon experiences, to give hints of its deepest dreams. But these dreams are not always fulfilled. The Disintegral also emerges later as the technical aspect of the psyche, the 'hacker' --- formerly called the 'dreamer' --- or the 'hierophant' --- that allows access to the most secret aspects of ourselves, often by connecting to its original sense of sacrifice, the sacrifice we have been experiencing in our lives::

Dreams (initial categories) -

Death or intelligence
Subliminal or lucid
Constructive or critical
New or young
Peaceful or textural
Open or closed
::

Dream Tectonics - I have mentioned
elsewhere in my entry under Mood Kinesthetic how moods are integrated with reality; Here, instead, the psyche is given
reign over things that might not be real;
Although, as psychology tells us, they are
certainly significant events; Coleridge
writes of having been influenced by a
dream during the writing of his short poem
Kubla Khan, and that he was an "opium-
eater"; We should not conclude that the
dream was in any degree less real, but
rather that there is an unconscious under-
tow, engendered perhaps in the earthy
physicalism of the drug; The layers of illusion that develop may sometimes by valuable to a poet, what may be called *illu-
siones plus fable*, but this has a way of
conceding the facts of the psyche; When
they are less unconscious, they are also
according to theory, more vulnerable to
conviction and paradox; Coleridge also reported that his marriage was unhappy and
he was rarely in good health; So, as in
waking life, there are two major compo-

nents to dreams: The conscious and the unconscious aspects; If it may be seen that only significant events cause conscious dreams, then it may also be derived that unconscious dreams are less diluted, and conscious dreams entail a certain degree of dangerous significance; Yet, other stipulations may be had: elaborate dreams may correspond to a developed brain (whether they are conscious or unconscious elaborations), and in some cases dreams may manifest simply because they are meaningless and it would make no difference to our energy; So there is a quadruple danger: (1) The unchecked power of the unconscious to control waking life, (2) The excessive significance of the consciousness of dreams, (3) The meaninglessness of lucid dreams, and (4) The potential meaninglessness of the entities of the psyche when conscious dreams have lost significance; So, the response to the dangers of dreams is fourfold also: (1) To be authentic to one's own sense of reasoning, (2) To take dreams 'with a grain of salt', (3) To pursue inner significance as a form of strength, and (4) To pursue outer significance to train the mind to be reasonable; Although some of these have a potential to perversify therapy, each of these steps counteracts the corresponding danger of the dreams themselves::

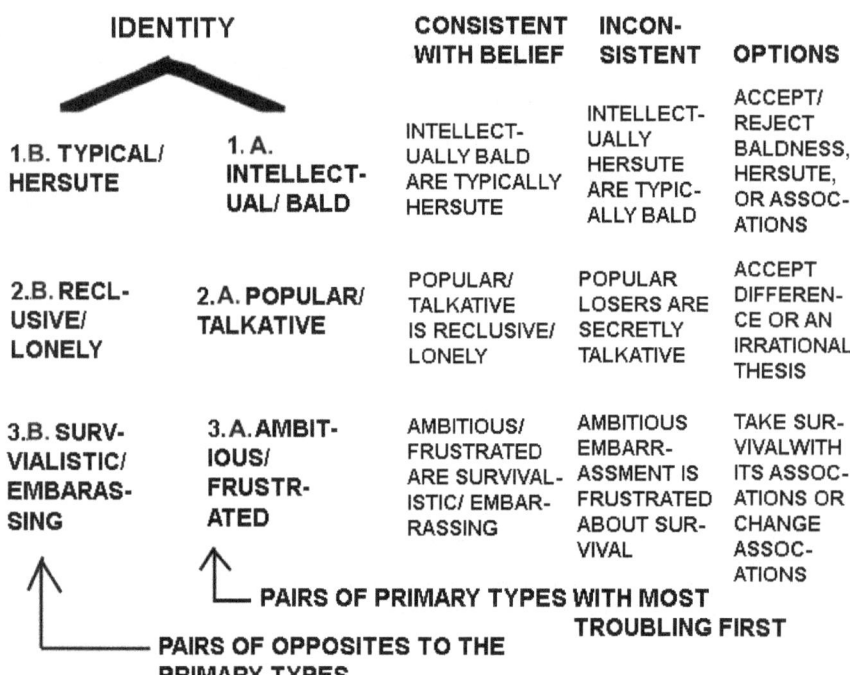

IDENTITY		CONSISTENT WITH BELIEF	INCON-SISTENT	OPTIONS
1.B. TYPICAL/ HERSUTE	1. A. INTELLECT-UAL/ BALD	INTELLECT-UALLY BALD ARE TYPICALLY HERSUTE	INTELLECT-UALLY HERSUTE ARE TYPIC-ALLY BALD	ACCEPT/ REJECT BALDNESS, HERSUTE, OR ASSOC-ATIONS
2.B. RECL-USIVE/ LONELY	2. A. POPULAR/ TALKATIVE	POPULAR/ TALKATIVE IS RECLUSIVE/ LONELY	POPULAR LOSERS ARE SECRETLY TALKATIVE	ACCEPT DIFFEREN-CE OR AN IRRATIONAL THESIS
3.B. SURV-VIALISTIC/ EMBARAS-SING	3. A. AMBIT-IOUS/ FRUSTR-ATED	AMBITIOUS/ FRUSTRATED ARE SURVIVAL-ISTIC/ EMBAR-RASSING	AMBITIOUS EMBARR-ASSMENT IS FRUSTRATED ABOUT SUR-VIVAL	TAKE SUR-VIVALWITH ITS ASSOC-ATIONS OR CHANGE ASSOC-ATIONS

PAIRS OF PRIMARY TYPES WITH MOST TROUBLING FIRST

PAIRS OF OPPOSITES TO THE PRIMARY TYPES

Dualistic Profile and Deductions -

A means of drawing conclusions from a patient's opinions;

Two alternatives at every level: accept your own beliefs and justifications, or change your view and find a new justifica-tion;

::

===============E================

Elapsion - figures prominently in the conjunction between interpersonal relations and problematics; People are adapted to expect that time will pass; There are multiple types of response to this: impatience, strategy, and boredom are examples; The critical insight, however, is that people are playing a game; They want others' efforts to materialize in a certain time frame, on an agenda they define themselves; Furthermore, these agendas interact, not only in terms of the agendas, but also in terms of the time frames; But if it is only a game, it still has rules; It is possible to find compatibility between what a patient person considers meaningless, and what the impatient person saves for later; Or between what the impatient person demands, and what a patient person has finally realized at the same time; Another possibility is the use of semantic concepts to re-define time boundaries; For example, what the patient person considers sacrosanct but impermanent may function for an impatient person's resolutions; But in the majority the subject of elapsion is one which concerns specific time frames which continually interact; Again, the corollary is authenticity, as it becomes drastically inefficient to misrepresent impatience, or to falsely represent a person's time premium; There is a precie to authentic versus inauthentic concepts of time::

83

Emotional Approach to Psychology and General Thesis - When philosophy is abstract and therefore virtual, psychology is emotional, and therefore involves a sensorium; Further, when philosophy could only apply value (ethics) to the problem of the experience machine, psychology can apply theories of meaning based on emotion; When philosophy, based on analogy, found meaning in opposites and consequently axiometry, psychology is free to establish a theory of similarity based on identity; Philosophically, psychology establishes that observable differences are real differences, although not always differences in motivation; Commonalities of location, language, and meaning often bind people together for purposes, occasions, and functions in which functional relationships develop, whether by identification or the desire for resemblance, with varying degrees of consciousness, and for a successful or unsuccessful purpose; Where people don't function, relationships disintegrate; Where identification is unconscious, little is realized; Where people identify, there is personal growth, yet where there is only a desire for resemblance, life is an artform rather than a society;

Therefore, alternatives:

1. A philosophy more integral than value
2. Psychology which may take emotion for granted

3. A metaphorical psychology
4. A psychology of motivations
5. A psychology of meaningful location
6. Otherwise, psychology is merely an art-form
::

Emotional Meaning -

Emotions are meaningful because they have meaningful objects. Meaningful objects can be thoughts about objects, purposes of objects, statements or beliefs about reality, or ultimately, holistic conditions-of-the-world. Depending on the theory of significance, one or more of these perspectives may be rejected, but the effect of rejecting one or more components may be to cause mental stress or physical frustration. For example, enjoying food may be meaningful in the sense that the food should not be completely ignored. However, indulging too much can be a scary experience, and a sign of obsession. This shows that with something as common as eating food, significance tends to determine how much we are allowed to indulge in the object of our experience. It is when the object is meaningless, and we are still obsessed, that the fear emerges. This may be traced to Eastern mystical notions of the illusion of the senses.

How much significance we can attach to our experiences depends on our level of satisfaction with abstract concepts of meaning. It may depend, for example, on the degree to which we use metaphor, symbolism, scientific interpretations, or creativity. It also depends on how deep our emotional experiences go: that is, how much pleasure and empathy we feel, how un-repressed we are with our sad or re-gretful feelings, how courageous or socia-ble we are, and how psychic or intelligent we are. Emotions do not necessarily de-pend on a theory of significance, at least not an overt one, but significance is a great help for finding coherence between our many experiences, and can offset madness, depression, vanity, and anger. Spiritual practitioners are often followers of one or another path of 'coherence' in the spiritual sense of the word, whereas scien-tists have adopted a critical type of coher-ence that also has its own brand of dapper emotionalism, often using wit to substitute for religious platitudes. Outside of religion and science, existentialists and other phi-losophers have sought their own sense of meaning as a function of intellect, often involving logical, metaphysical, and ethical belief systems.

Emotional Tranquilizer - In the figurative sense, tranquilizers are assumptions or attitudes which stultify emotion; These may be adopted by the patient as a way of suppressing or coping, and may be adopted by the professional as an unnecessary countermeasure to what might otherwise be genuine realizations; Sometimes, however, tranquilizers serve as a desirable bastion of strength in the therapy experience; It then must be judged when a tranquilizer is tactful, relative to the *necessity* of realization; In this utility, a certain amount of standard self-questioning may be effective, but not to the point where it tires the patient; Various levels of emotional testament are possible, as shown below in the diagram (these are examples, not exclusive cases. See also the appendix under Emotional Language Techniques):

Tranquilized

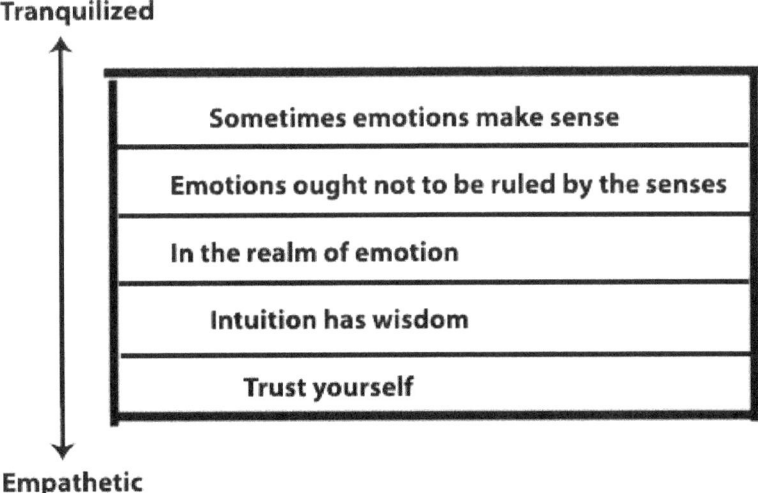

Sometimes emotions make sense

Emotions ought not to be ruled by the senses

In the realm of emotion

Intuition has wisdom

Trust yourself

Empathetic

Emotions - Real emotions can be built from virtual emotions and manifested values; Values are discovered by experience, and have no definite emotion;

Virtual Emotions

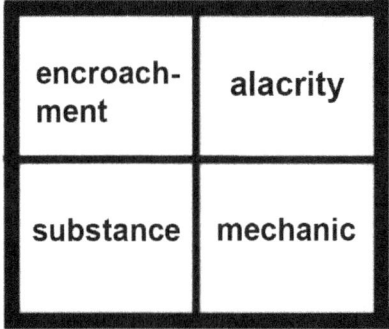

encroach-ment	alacrity
substance	mechanic

Although these have sometimes played a role in formulating empathy, they are often inauthentic and insincere; Alacrity is the sense of having emotion 'on the tip of one's tongue'; Encroachment is confidence about emotion; Substance is merely a sense of the presence of people or things; Mechanic is the capability to produce a new feeling, which is not yet tangible; Collectively, the effect is of a large swath of possible 'virtual feelings'::

Ethos of Madness -

In some cases, specific phrases introduced in early development can prevent
illness such as paranoid schizophrenia or
schizo-affective disorder by re-wiring per-
suasions; This is especially true if the individual has strong motivations or a willingness to understand others; Even if the illness is not cured, some disasters may be
prevented; Here are some simple phrases
to illicit epiphanies against madness:

"What is more important than paranoia,
and what is more useless?"

"What is more important than madness is
sanitation, and caring for yourself"

"Think about it: functional madness is always less than totally mad"

"No one knows what the mad man knows:
not even the mad man"

::

Exceptional Psychology -

Perfectly unexcept- ional	That's the way it happens
Then you change your mind	Time to do the grown- up thing

This may be called 'the path that everyone follows', ostensibly because it is so functional; The categories equally capture love, intellectual ambition, and suicide; The difference, apparently, is the treatment of the third category; Essentially, artificial judgments---judgments which create an opinion without an undeniable foundation--- should be avoided, and doing so prevents suicide; That is the sheerly abstract position on the negative side of exceptional psychology::

Existential Parallels of Madness -

EXISTENTIAL PARALLELS OF MADNESS

Existence	Mindset	Parallel/Idea	Contingency/Risk
Existential reality	Existential sanity	Survival	Optimization
Mental reality	Mental sanity	Coherence	Systemization
Parallel reality	Parallel sanity	Correspondence	Personalization
Contingent reality	Contingent sanity	Utility	Idealization
Quasi-reality	Quasi-sanity	Reasoning	Concern
Dangerous reality	Dangerous sanity	Responsibility	Morality

Expressing gradations; If we see how an individual person is not ever purely dangerous or in some way non-existent, these comparisons express how, working from the bottom, the irrational person argues out of a sense of idealization, whereas the psychologist, if he argues, must argue from the top, out of a sense of optimization; The psychologist's understanding of survival is at odd ends with the irrational fascination; In fact, what this shows is that the irrational are not so irrational after all; For every contingent sanity, there is a contingent reality, and that is not even the worst case; Fortunately, every kind of person is a kind of optimum, so we can say that in some sense, the parallel of many contingencies expressed by survival, opti-

91

mum, cohering, system, correspondence, personality, utility, and idealization (and in the worst cases reasoning, concern, responsibility, morality), allows a wide range of inherent functional behaviors, which may oftentimes be unconscious or contractual; Interpreting these aspects further, there is a relativistic advantage in adopting madness as the standard of ordinary imperfect situations, so long as the madness is understood in the abstract::

Extensive Space - Although I have made efforts to avoid obstreperous conceptual instruments, I think it is important to introduce extensive space as a concept to psychology, particularly because it allows some associations with the theory of resemblance, and my attempt to develop a theory of coherent psychology; Although this development seems fundamentally basic, incidentally it leads into studies of higher intelligence and higher forms of life; So in my view the study is warranted, not just for typical reasons, but for humanistic ones;

Extension exists in multiple degrees, which can be called modes, as shown in the first row of the diagram; In the second row are the most fundamental objects which refer to that form of extension---(whether they are mental constructs or purely material); The objects refer to the type of insight which corresponds to each degree of ex

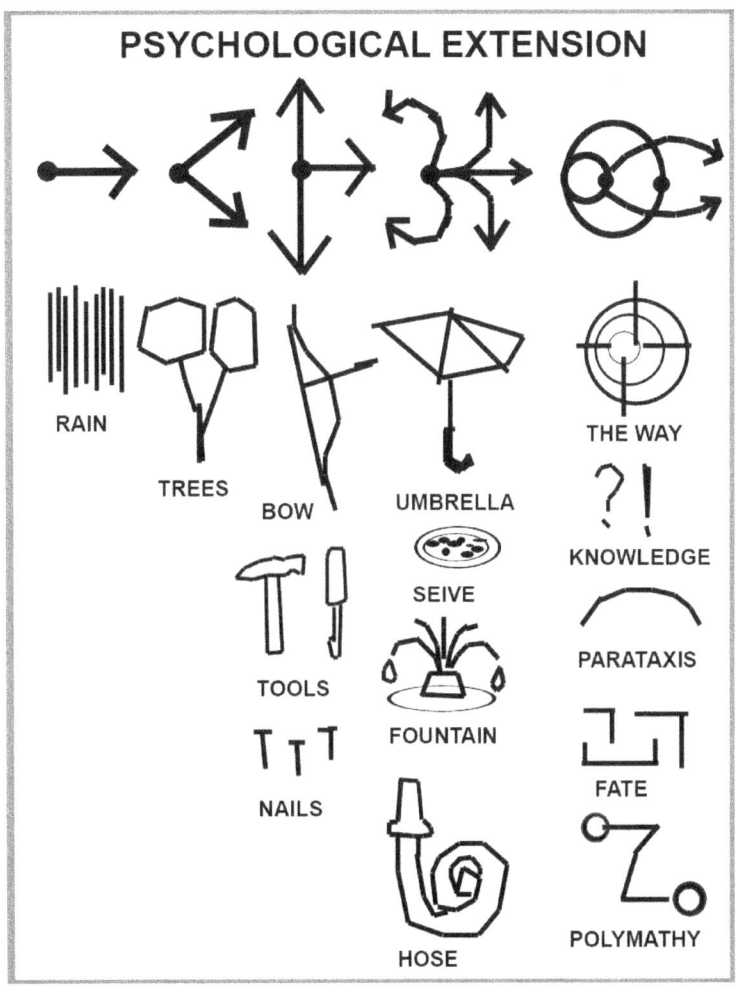

PSYCHOLOGICAL EXTENSION

RAIN

TREES

BOW

UMBRELLA

SEIVE

TOOLS

NAILS

FOUNTAIN

HOSE

THE WAY

KNOWLEDGE

PARATAXIS

FATE

POLYMATHY

tension; Thus, if earlier forms are simpler, they are also more common, and thus prone to greater misconception when used in large quantity; Later stages are more advanced but also exist in larger quantities;

A simple sketch of the use of the categories is to establish that labels which refer to stages of development also may refer to more than one stage of the diagram; For example, in the context of education, we might have the set (1) Child, (2) Student, (3) Professor, (4) Emeritus; We can say that the existential stages which refer for example to the child polymath (1.1-5.5) might be higher than the stage of a student with tools (1.2-3.2); A similar example is another set: (1) confusion, (2) construction, (3) innovation, (4) invention; The invention of rain might be lower than the construction of a hose, but innovation with trees might be equal in level to construction of fountains; What is most helpful psychologically is not only that these provide access to thoughts about development, but that these stages are highly symbolic of real thought-processes which exist in the world; The existence of the stages of development 'as thoughts' establishes their psychological validity; As is usual for this precise type of analysis, the result is a suggestion of levels beyond the human::

===============F=================

Father Narrative - often exists mostly in women's minds, by women's thoughts, and it is this life of thought which in the majority is interpreted and read by children; Not only does the female narrative remain invisible and mysterious, but the father narrative may itself not reflect reality; Therefore the children face a double delusion, which does much of the work in defining the rationality of choices which emerge at and immediately after adolescence; In some ways, the intimidation produced by this wall of intrigue does much to explain why individuals do not mature earlier than they do; While the father humbles himself with an idealization of his self-perceptions, the same delusions may appear grandiloquently in the woman's mind, as a kind of delinquent charade or sad masquerade which, while in some respects less delusional, is also prone to misinterpretations in its assumed context, which may be one of social communiqués; Girls famously can carry the narrative whether or not their father is intelligent, employed, or even living; This goes to show that the female narrative is something more powerful than the male's, and also that the earlier-mentioned perceptions of men are mostly a creation of the mind, however powerful they are; What may be a women's insight is that men are infinitely reducible and susceptible to criticism; From her point, however, the father narrative is a form of realism, if only ultimately because it provides a character of explanation; If the woman chooses to be philosophical, the explanation could be arbitrary; The entire male narrative is contingent upon communication, or perhaps God ---some idea that amuses those who take interest in men; And it is not that the contingency does service; It is more like men are products of free-association than communication or God; Yet these concepts remain important for interpretation::

Fault of Perception - Particular patients have trouble with this area, asking: 'How is the individual to blame?' or even 'How is it about me?' or 'It isn't just something that happened?'; The case becomes serious when something serious is implicated, but the patients often don't seem to realize it; Both hindsight and foresight become limited; For example, the question can be raised that 'Some motorcycle accidents go unreported'; The fault of perception raises the idea that unreported accidents are somehow unreal; In a similar way, someone may be tempted to think that extramarital relations do not raise typical problems, or conversely, that their own person is always as good as statistics; In fact, neither of the statements is true; Enforcing the concept of realism may often involve raising the question of faulty perception as a minimum; In some cases, without the right background, a client may fall into patterns of behavior that would be avoidable with a slight alteration of perspective; This may be the case for example, with under-age drinking and drug use; The utility, then, is to avoid the contended territory called 'mistakes'::

Fear - Basis of -

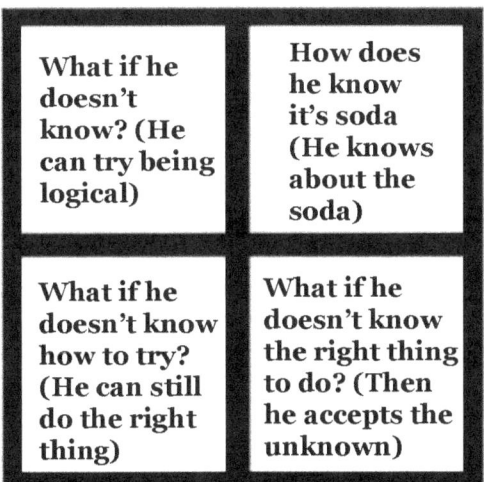

The relation to depression and panic disorders can be seen in the final two questions;

There is a pattern that emerges that knowledge *should* but does not resolve the problem of fear; I still think knowledge is

97

underrated in the solution, but there is a degree of emotionalism that is also implied; When this emotion means fear, this can be resolved by distinguishing between internal or external conflicts, and combining practical optimism with any emergent theory, or else applying a method that is less abstract;

The remaining dilemma is that physical problems may have an abstract solution, as in arachnophobia, and abstract problems may have a physical solution, as in basic fear, and that abstractions sometimes involve physical connotations for their reality, while physical things may seem to have divine authority; Part of the solution, as mentioned earlier, is to discriminate if they are one thing or the other (physical or abstract): then intellectual choice may result in an intellectual ailment, and a physical choice may result in a real problem; But at least there is a choice; However, as a function of conditioning, there may not be a choice;

So, the first solution to fear is knowledge, the second is emotional adjustment, the third is honest opinion, and the fourth is determination::

Fetishistic Determinism - Explains why many objects have appeal when the person cannot necessarily argue for the object's purpose, significance, or appeal; On the one hand, the appeal of objects may lie in a general system, such as thought, society, or aesthetics; But such an approach risks alienating the object from its own significance; A more accurate approach might be to postulate that objects reciprocate with the mind; Either the object has proven significance in this process, or the mind must determine an arbitrary significance for the object; Otherwise, we are defending a disembodied theory or a dysfunctional mind; The most conservative choice appears to be arbitrary significance, which leaves us with the theory that the value of objects is often made up by fetishistic determinism: the ascription of arbitrary properties made up by the mind for the purposes of producing significance, a form of non-objective functionalism::

Fine Motor Skills - develop very early in some children, perhaps at birth, with the stipulation that the early motions of the arm and fingers are designations of a kind of significance nearly identical to the individual's selective pattern in graphic control later in life;

Experiences with architecture (such as traveling the world or having picture books

read to them) and watching time-lapse vid-
eos---and other technical animations such
as wire-frames, illustrations, and comparisons between sketches and photographs--
-has the potential to increase graphical
skill and create a technical correspoend-
ence between the infant's arm motions
and, as it were, the entire world;

These developments, mostly experiences-
of-experiences involving media, or also
exceptional extensions of experience itself
---such as atmospheric locations, music, or
later sex---also contribute to the mediality
or interfaced quality of life, with potential
applications in neurology, social media,
and virtual reality;

The adult's experience of engaging with
media---as it has been documented in relation to sex and other phenomena---often
dates back to early experiences of en-
gagement with the world; Studying the role
these moments of learning play in relation
to specific instances such as fine motor
function has potential to expand the understanding of emotional-technical connection
and the larger framework of human significance in general;

Studies are already being done for example, on the subject of haptics and learning,
and the role of personality upon habit formation; Clearly these would be interesting
to develop in a genetic or sensorium context, where the association for specific

body movements can be expanded into an alethic system::

Found Psychology - has an underrated presence, particularly if aspects such as color and texture are adequate to switch a mood completely in other directions; Without some experiment this may seem near-impossible, but under what some call luxury treatment, beginning with an absence of bare walls or the presence of genuinely soothing music---music that does not inspire agony---such a texture of feeling may seem possible; It may often rely on a level of specificity that is uncommon even in artistic endeavors, but this must not make it impossible; There may even be common traits of neurosis or agony which lend themselves to this purpose; In the first place, the qualities of the texture are simply those which do not inspire agony: curves or homeliness may be desirable, with some modification; In some cases only specific photographs or the chosen colors of a mental hospital will do; The reassurance may be secondary to an encroaching fear that these objects could be lost; The patient may be reassured by solid objects, durable cloth, and references to inner processes; It may help to integrate with the patient (responsibly), a process he or she fully expects; In general, however, the texture amounts to the following:

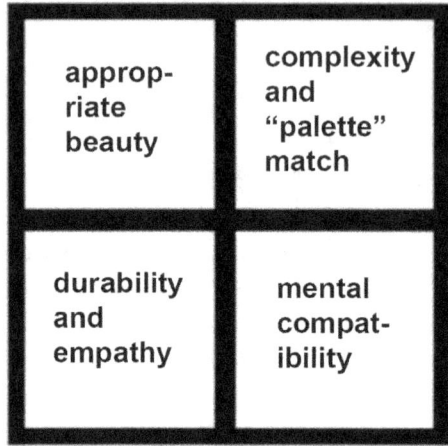

These routes may seem excessive in a high-tolerance situation, if such exists, but in the case of schizophrenia there is often a high degree of sensitivity which becomes intolerable if conditions are not met, even if those conditions seemexorbitant, it may be possible to meet the patient half-way, or even, with little expense, to make a tolerable impression; Clearly this kind of expectation with treatment lays a foundation for the more general use of emotional textures to please nearly anyone, and thus to contribute to prevention of many of the mild malaises and nuanced intolerances which contribute to mental syndromes::

Freud, Sigmund - The most famous of psychologists, he made famous the concepts of death and sex drives, and organized psychotherapy around the theme of

an incest complex; Noted for his pessimism in later life, he nonetheless has a
strong influence in the work of Jung, Otto,
Adler, and those who came after them::

Fullrich Effect - The theory beginning with
Freud that people are composed of inade-
quacies; An example is that the tongue
has not grown to fit inside the nose, or
sexual fetishes ultimately express abnormal function; Although partly ameliorated
by norms and relativistic morality, it may
still be shown that at least in a physical
and absurdist sense human life is composed of partial solutions; Essentially this
implicates a mathematical view of life::

Future Psychology can be interpreted by
several methods; The first is fairly simple:
(1) Take psychology in general and add a
category that has not been used before, or
(2) Make psychology apply to a new ex-
perimental context, or (3) Begin with a
context outside of psychology, and make it
psychological, or (4) Apply 'Meta' or 'Post'
to a discipline and apply it to psychology;

Examples:

*Media psychology, post-political psychol-
ogy, integrational psychology, boundary
psychology;*

That is the most typical method; Another

method is: (1) Find a previous example of psychology and develop it, or (2) Find the opposite of the same example, or (3) Create a new context for the same example (and apply it to psychology), or (4) Find an opposite for a new context of the same example;

Examples of this method are the following:

1. Behaviorism --> Situationism
2. Behaviorism --> Relative psychology,
       or, Situationism -->
       Contemplative psychology
3. Contemplative psychology --> Con
              templative media,
       or, Relative psychology --> True
                       objects
4. Contemplative media --> Processes
              of inhibition
       or, True objects --> Artificial
                       synthesis

In these descriptions alone, there are two quasi-exclusive contexts of ideas, only a quarter of which may be utterly familiar:

[Example 1]

True Objects	Behavior-ism
Relative Psych-ology	Artificial Synthesis

[Example 2]

Contemp-lative Media	Situation-ism
Contemp-lative Psy-chology	Processes of Inhib-ition

Although other translations are possible, this gives some idea of a method that can be used to find creative areas of research::

===============G===============

(A) **Generative Language Disorder** typically occurs when there is limited control of
subject matter; So, for example, if the setting includes a muddy road and people are
being covered with it because they can't
dig out, and also the topic of people comes
up, which may or may not be inevitable,
then people are forced to conjoin---
consciously or unconsciously---the
phrases 'mud' and 'people'; The result is
the phrase 'mud people'; In subsequent
conversations it may be unavoidable to
think of people in general or especially the
same people, as mud people, even though
the mud may not have been under individual control; Even that incident might be
called a generative language disorder
(mild signs of which do not usually mean a
serious illness), but often the cases are
less literal, creating a potentially confusing
problem; Someone may obsess with subjects such as 'fuck' and 'shit' because
these topics have been introduced in that
manner, even in small forms; The subliminal content, just as in the case of mud, is
often swallowed in its entirety, producing
disturbing patterns of unconscious
thoughts ('what if the mud eats me', 'what
if everyone is gay'); What is important to
realize is that the individual is not wholly
responsible for these thoughts; Therefore,
in all mature and functional instances there

will be some control over them (or the therapist can say that someone is 'being immature'); But that is not to say that the thoughts don't exist; It is merely that they are being suppressed or 'put through a lens'; In some cases , in the case of highly disturbing images for example, a lens will not be enough to eliminate the problem, and strange instances of assumptions will begin to appear in language; In such a case, if functionality is affected it might be called a neurosis, and treated through suppression, immersion, or medication, and other specific methods such as language control::

Gestalt Psychology - A school with at least applicational significance founded in Germany by Wertheimer, and often faulted for its complexity; Essentially, it was learned that through some perhaps unknown intuitive process, animals such as humans could make a quantum leap from one basic set of cognitive organization to a much more complex set; This can be demonstrated by classification stratagems and optical illusions; The Gestalt insight that the whole is more than the part is even said to apply to moral theories; Gestalt theories provide a basis motivation for reward systems which boost creativity; Evidence that punishment is more structuring brings criticism when it is evidently structure which creates classification stratagems; Thus there are a number of options:

(1) In an ideal case, punishment occurs in a value system, a non-physical punishment system, and subsequently creativity is proportional to reward, interpreted broadly to include the pre-conditions of intelligence, (2) Creativity is a 'natural number' so that creativity is not proportional to punishment, (3) Objective structures exist which are uncovered by 'insight' or intelligence, independent of reward or punishment; intelligence is objectivity, or (4) While punishment creates categories, intelligence makes better use of them; the fault with intelligence and behavior is the brutality enacted upon it; Because the selections seem limited to contexts such as these, Gestalt theory has drawn considerable criticism; However, my thesis of Gestalt theory remains that intelligence develops organically, so that optical illusions are really a function of development and not some 'innate idea'; A secondary thesis is that specific gestalt adaptations are 'situated in nature', so that intelligence scales to the available dimensions of nature::

Good and Evil (Psychological Concept of) - This is reached by the Integrator, a relatively advanced concept of personality. Less advanced stages of personality might better be treated as 'bad' and 'good,' (blame and reward), or 'pleasant' and 'unpleasant' --- this last set of choices being very appropriate for short attention spans, and often working with reinforcement. Blame and reward is most successful when it is accepted by the individual, but is not at all functional when it is not accepted. The sense in which resistance may replace principle becomes dangerous if reward and punishment is seen as the only means of influencing someone::

==============H==============

Habitualism - is the natural mien of most therapists, for reasons that may be well-founded; A patient should be relaxed when receiving care and concern, and often-times experienced expertise depends on methods which are tried and true; However, at the same time, habitualism is a subtle demon of psychology; Perhaps the most consistent demon to go unquestioned as an implement, or at least a recurrent subtlety of therapy relationships; Patients often do not identify with a therapist's self-satisfaction, or if they do, expect some doctrine or special message to reinforce an emotional plateau; Habitualism is against both of these things; So, therefore, from a dimensional point of view it is necessary to interpret habits in a way that responds to those specific difficulties::

Happiness -

Studies of Happiness

Assuming the two contexts (diagonals) represent opposites, two forms of categorical deduction are produced: 'happy is happier and a pessimist is happy that you're happy', or 'being happy that you're happy is happier, and happiness is pessimism';

The two options are happiness and pessimism, but the two options are ever-present; In the first case what is presented is an objective relative case, such as one person to another; (Happiness is the subject of the frequent adage that one could always find someone else who is more miserable); The second is different, and less competitive, or perhaps self-competitive; In the second case, happiness seems to involve some analysis, or at least an identification that happiness and pessimism are part of the same condition; What is advocated is either advantage or neutrality::

================I===============

Idealization - The idealization of the external runs the risk of belittling the internal parts of reality. Yet if, between two iinternals, one is already better treated, then it is narcissistic to declare that the exterior of the other is being idealized, since it may be that the one that is not idealized feels worse.

Imprecision - Is the primary power of child intelligence. Through this power of the most general type of intelligence, children can associate broadly and think powerfully. The power of imprecision, however, often hits a roadblock when it attempts to summon the energy to express itself. Imprecision is often confused by the child with other concepts, particularly questioning, and in some children, criticism. Although criticism may by a choice that ultimately pays off for academic opportunities, in some ways it is a compromised position. Further, criticism is also in debt to the questioning process, and questioning is by no means the only form of generalism. Some fortunate children are raised with the more psychologically appropriate focus on 'Being' as the nature of generality. Although a better life-choice, sometimes the focus on being leaves the child with specious generalities that are incommunicable. However, via questions or some other perspectivism, imprecision remains a powerful tool for child intelligence. Combined with several other tools, such as mental pleasure, curiosity, set ups, and science vs. mystery, imprecision may remain useful well into the developing years, and perhaps beyond, with enough interest.

Improviso - is a character more social, or initially social, than the Apercu and the Permiscu; Here is a psychological entity that depends on what I call 'elabora' or the process of convocation; Improviso exists superficially as unrealized relationships; It also exists in a fixed form in relationships that are prescribed; Although it manifests as a form of desire, it is not inherently emotional; On first impression or first inclination, the form varies; On second inclination, there is a correspondence between simple and complex relationships, a desire to know the 'underlying thing' whatever it is; It may seem like curiosity, but it is actually motivated by desire, and still deeper by the underlying fabric of life; At this stage it may be seen that informal relationships have hidden formalities, and the character of the Improviso may even be highly contingent; It is in the contingent form that the Improviso is most interesting; For example, the influence female opinion plays on the Father Narrative may seem like truth in a male position, whereas a woman notices its contingent dependence on language and female narrative; Because of its complexity, it is always impor-

113

tant to interpret the condition of the improviso before deciding that it is understood;
While the contingent view of the Improviso
in this case could be abbreviated as social
aptitude, it is also possible that social aptitude can be abbreviated as a contingency,
creating a further recess that may depend
on structures such as language, and factu-
ality; In this sense irreducible processes
may define the Improviso::

Inductive Psychology (Primary Form of)
-

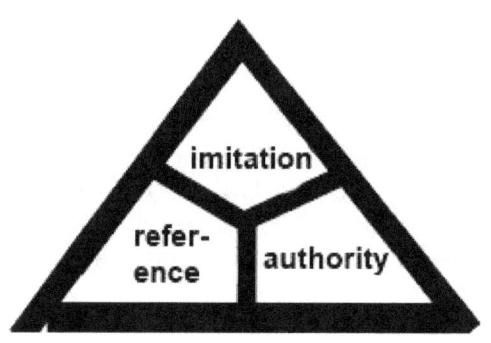

Inductive psychology seeks some means
of inference, such as imitation, reference,
or authority; When some have assumed
the social function of induction it may
sometimes be noted that what is adopted
is a mere social formality; It is not always
clear what category such a social formal-
ism belongs to, whether it is an abstract
authority, a qualified reference such as
that coming from therapeutic experience,
or instead a variation on an imitative pat-

tern; The three categories provide a means for comparing and contrasting alternate definitions of psychological induction or inference::

Information Thesis - Part 1: See Consummate Information, Part 2: See Psychic Facts::

The Innuendo - I define as 'The most direct explanation of a thing'; This seems parallaxial, because after all a lot of means of explanation converge on a single object being explained; Thus we must reject all forms of complex evidence *unless* it is decided that complexity itself serves a purpose for the object; The clearest expression of this is to separate the idea of a thing from any complex system that we would otherwise assume useful; But, deceptively, no arbitrary system exists either; Therefore we must be guided by the exact terms of the evidence; While in philosophy direct evidence may not be desirable, because it may be subjective, in psychology there is something to be said for direct perceptions; Questions are immediately raised, such as 'Is it sinful to view/ understand an object?', 'Am I as I appear to be?', 'Am I only what I understand, and not what my ego tells me I am?'; In any case, although the hypotheses may be strange, they are honest assessments of thought, perhaps the only types of perceptions available to those under psychic stress; Thus, understanding or performing

115

under the conditions of a patient's thoughts may be the only way to move on and recover; The innuendo may be a distant truth which science is unable to discover, or it may be a reflection of an inner self declaring its own sense of adequate needs; Certainly, those two choices may be seen as exclusive, since what is not desirable to the self must be outside the desirable self: when the self is desirable the observed object is always understandable as either an aspect of psychic desire or an aspect of the world-problem; And unless the world is unsolvable, there is direct compatibility between the self and the world, when the self has been granted this degree of understanding::

Insanity Thesis - It may be said that no one lacks basic motivation unless there is a problem with function; Traditionally these types are divided into three categories: handicapped, irrational, or depressed; Depending on the context, some of these types may have an additional criterion of confusion, which is associated with the specific case of dysfunction (e.g. one of these three categories); Sometimes confusion is associated with physical degeneration, suggesting that it is not psychological in nature, or at least that the circumstance can be proven to be environmental or environmental-conceptual (my thesis of dementia); Irrationality such as psychosis falls into several categories of motivation, based on this diagram:

Motiv-ated	Basically
Psych-ologic-ally	Insane

(Read CCW from upper right)

In the first case (1) The individual only has to meet basic needs unless the definition of these needs changes, so basic needs will be met even with psychosis, if there is a recovery period (that is, unmedicated recoveries are possible in basic areas, as has been widely reported, but this does not affect dangerous dysfunctions); (2) The individuals' motivations, if rational, will not be irrational, but may be instead dysfunctional---individuals frequently will hold onto a thread of reasoning or significance, which does not disappear; This is highly contextual, requiring empathy; (3) When the individual expresses psychological sophistication, this will not disappear, although the individual may become more or less conscious of that; (4) Insanity itself, if functional, is functional, it is only dysfunctional insanity that seems to lack genuine motivation (ignoring some relativity);

To sum up, in the context of motivation, insanity must be treated as an independent variable; Individuals under treatment may be capable of profound yet dysfunctional behaviors, which may have function in a context of dysfunction (in some cases, the patient may have more understanding than the clinical staff, especially when specific circumstances are considered); The individual is always motivated to meet basic needs, unless the definition of those needs has changed; The easier it is to meet basic needs, the more likely these needs will be met, independent of insanity; This final statement leads to my conclusion, that insanity is essentially an exacerbated needs problem tangled up with the highly contextual problem of understanding; If this seems too beggarly, we would do to reflect on our assumptions of the limitations of such individuals, who surely in some cases are deserving of privileges for which they would be grateful::

The Integrator - Functional beings always go through an early stage of integration, which may be their extraordinary learning experiences, their emotional relationships, or their sense of dedication to some purpose. Not everyone is so lucky. Many other people seek after this stage desperately, often losing ground in a struggle to realize even small fragments of what seems like daily business to those who are functional. I made two critical insights about this stage: (1) This stage is preceded by a stage called The Unitarian, the success of which depends on frank, casual assessment of what is necessary for functionality. This earlier stage is easier for some than for others. (2) The Integrator is much easier to reach with frank assessment of the qualities of good and evil, ideally with enough common sense not to make mistakes. Now it can be seen that the Integrator may be characterized as being over-responsible, but in return it receives many rewards. It writes off the kinds of problems which the neurotic encounters in his own mind, and the result is a shortcut to success. While there are more functional types, they often embracing specific roles in the context of life choices, with good or evil results::

Interpretation, Forms of-

Forms of Interpretation, Lower Form of:

Forms of interpretation could obviously involve the entire list under Social Psychology, but it may be convenient to have a narrower list, and to render it categorical:

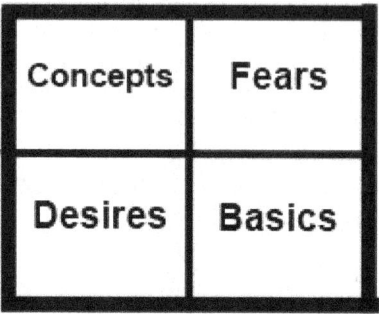

Concepts	Fears
Desires	Basics

Here the greatest potential for complexification occurs in the fourth stage where 'basic' may be subject to re-definition, affecting the rest of the diagram; Consequently the following may be more sufficient where a new definition is necessary:

Forms of Interpretation, Upper Form of:

Modes	Conser-vations
Impuls-ivity	Systems

Here it may be adequate to treat 'systems' as social psychology, and leave the remainder utterly independent; The result, as with the previous, is a holistic approach;

For example of holistics, it can be

schemed out that there are lessons to be learned from this second context: 'modes refer to systems, and impulses refer to conservations (also called loyalties)'; 'Unless modes are systems, impulses aren't conservative': that is where problems emerge, under a theory that any illness involves some responsibility (the 'impulse' for disease)::

Intransible Faculty - An important notion in thought and psychology, that an aspect of perception or process may become fixed in the mind, so as to produce a consistent conditioned response, conviction, or unfulfilled motivation; It is reasonable to suppose that such a faculty serves a functional purpose; For example, it may be important in recording key memories and therefore instantiating a sense of self-purpose; Or it may serve as a working platform in which one fixed concept is traded for another; This could influence the structure of thoughts and the development of intelligent approaches to functionalistic problems; But does it pose a moral difficulty?; Can those with an intransible faculty be developed personalities?; The result of the second question may depend on identification; Perhaps contingent to any notion of knowledge, the individual must represent aspects of his or her experience; If that is not true, a conflict is created; And if it is true, there may be some factor which triggers disproportionate representation, including an obsessive

121

intransible faculty; What about morality?;
Normatively, environment instantiates
what it means to have an obsession; If environment is unknown psychologically or
literally, obsessions become less tractable;
Objectively, knowledge of a client's inner
landscape, his or her preferences or desires, creates a context for any knowledge
of their intransible faculty::

Itineralism (also Itinerantism) - as opposed to Aspiantialism, the ability to provide meaning for general procedures or
large numbers of actions; Historically, this
has often been ascribed to religious
thought, social philosophy, or general expertise; However, the term itineralism provides additional insight: that such systems
or forms of mindfulness may be constructive (iterative or translational) or in some
way aggregative or componential, much in
the way of the synergist; These point towards a distinct psychological faculty such
as memory or the amygdala as a source
for the meaning of general procedures;
(See opposite at Aspiantialism)::

===============J===============

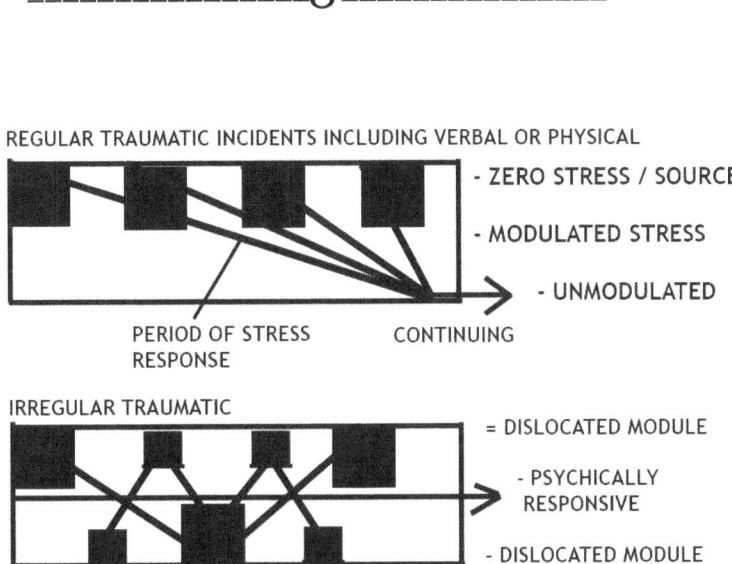

REGULAR TRAUMATIC INCIDENTS INCLUDING VERBAL OR PHYSICAL

- ZERO STRESS / SOURCE

- MODULATED STRESS

- UNMODULATED

PERIOD OF STRESS RESPONSE   CONTINUING

IRREGULAR TRAUMATIC

= DISLOCATED MODULE

- PSYCHICALLY RESPONSIVE

- DISLOCATED MODULE

CONFUSED, BASED ON RESEMBLANCES

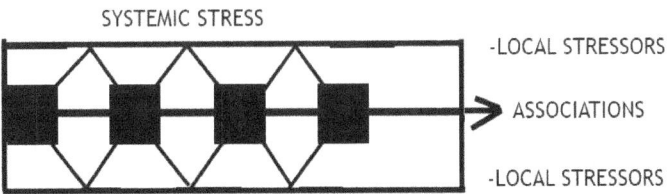

SYSTEMIC STRESS

-LOCAL STRESSORS

ASSOCIATIONS

-LOCAL STRESSORS

Jung, Carl - The major progenitor of archetypal studies in psychology, and with Freud, one of the two major traditional theorists about the unconscious; He is

123

known as the founder of cognitive psychology, emphasizing the importance of dreams; In his Man and His Symbols and the Red Book he details the importance of symbolism and love respectively; Although meaning was an important aspect of Jung's work, universalism was a psychological dimension for Jung; Although he worked to radically re-define the working definition of psychology, the acceptability of a universal system of meaning was one of Jung's unrealized legacies::

===============L===============

A **Lapsodic Pattern** is observed especially in a patient's coping with traumatic
data; The data is explicated by reasoning
in degrees of difference from the ordinary;
Thus patterns develop between major and
minor stressors; These instances of
trauma, if regular, are treated as examples
of ordinary events; In such a case the diagram showing a lapsodic pattern indicates
a dwindling of basic stress response and
an increase of psychic stress, shown by a
continuing and un-modulated form of
stress; If irregular, a similar diagram may
show the last traumatic event, indicating
that similarities confirm stress, while time
dilutes it; In this case the psychic stress is
more pragmatic and responsive, what
might be called modulated psychic stress;

LAPSODIC PATTERNS

LAPSODIC PATTERN AND TEMPORALITY

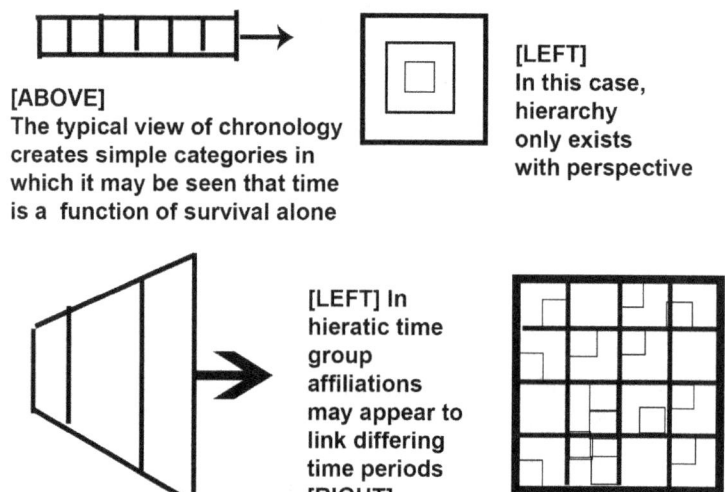

[ABOVE]
The typical view of chronology creates simple categories in which it may be seen that time is a function of survival alone

[LEFT]
In this case, hierarchy only exists with perspective

[LEFT] In hieratic time group affiliations may appear to link differing time periods **[RIGHT]**

MOVING LAPSODIC PATTERN:
If motion were possible through time, the lapsodic pattern might differ from standard chronology by creating specific and general forms of time, both of which may have standard-independent ranges of motion; In other words, top-down perspective may be inappropriate::

Lapsodic Pattern and Temporality
: :

Laughter - A well-placed laugh can reduce time in a mental institution, and even in some cases prevent someone from being committed in the first place; That is, especially when laughter is considered a part of the complex of functional behaviors; In this role considerable, perhaps unreasonable tact is involved on the part of the 'patient'; There are many reported cases of laughter combined with limited dysfunctional behavior being grounds for additional psychiatric help, hospitalization, or even police attention; This occurs especially in schools, where conformity is at a premium; Increasingly young people seem to have to pay invisible prices to venture into creative activities at all (qua 'institutionalization'); This is even visible very early, in the sand box, and with building blocks, where child care staff may show impatience and expect children to follow a prescribed procedure which thereby becomes substantively less symbolic or merely represents a negotiation with authorities; Indeed, humor itself has been hard to buy, and is increasingly of a manufactured variety, including artificial values such as trendiness and the appearance of conforming to the competitive culture of stand-up comedy routines; There is a rumor that humor, like creativity, lacks a

127

soul; That is the root cause and explanation for the difficulty in applying humor to
mental health; Proving that one has a
sense of humor becomes a task as difficult
as changing someone's self-serving opinion; The establishment seems to accept
only branded personalities; Nor is it necessary to stomach originality in the history of
rhetorical exchanges; History seems only
to accept strong personalities that don't
make excuses, and then to brand the folly
that results when the conformity is imperfect or even criminal; Indeed, strength
without a crime is a strange power that
teenagers may not understand; Whatever
the answer is---whether it is passive
strength, or some kind of incident or ex-
ception---it says something about the nature conflicts such as the Oedipus complex; In this context, humor is a secret,
powerful art, that only in the best cases (or
not the worst ones) refers to genuine good
nature or health; If older generations take
this sour side of humor for granted, certainly it is worth re-iterating that these people have noticed its cruelty and competi-
tiveness; It is something like the idea that
stand-up comedy has become a common
value, and fortunately, a value that may be
modified to various levels of audiences;
Otherwise, the choice is to present humor,
irony, value, folly, or to be mocked; Incidentally, these become significant ideas of
the character of populations under the influence of the norm of laughter::

Laws of Frustration - Frustration, under the view that it coincides with maddening aspects, corresponds with several things: (1) The Collective Impression, (2) Uncertainty or Ambiguity, (3) Nit-Picking, and (4) Arbitrary Tough Decisions. It may then be seen that depending on the personality, solving frustration (perhaps even madness), involves solving one or more than one of these four aspects. A general program for solving frustration might then involve (1) Eliminating nightmares resulting from ambiguity, (2) Making life easier to reduce tough decisions, (3) Promoting creativity and independence, or in other ways giving a platform for decision-making, and (4) Providing meaningful information on simple, intermediate, and complex levels specifically for the purpose of allowing individuals to have a positive, meaningful, and coherent view of reality.

Literal Delusion - A potential limitation of the professional view of delusions is the willingness to take a patient literally; Although on matters of fact, literalism is highly useful, there is no guarantee that a client or patient is being literal in everything he or she says; If we are certain that the client is honest, there is no reason to limit honesty to known territories or working tools; I suspect there is no handicap of a person's associations by the expected bounds of imagination, or even the known laws of nature; Indeed, what a person

genuinely intends may have a highly specific meaning to him or her; What a patient
intends (apart from the unconscious or social anxiety) has often been a neglected
area in psychology, and yet has much to
say about psychological development and
motivation; So long as the psychologist
understands that a patient can be complex, however, it seems justified to use
some variation of the literal view of the unconscious: this reflects the therapist's
rather than the patient's honesty::

Literalistic Darwinism - The state that
determines that non-literalism is a secondary characteristic; The social psychology
of truth, real or non-existent; The assumption of connotative relevance; The over-
bearing need for language; The manipulation of the mind by non-entities; The calcu-
lus of normalcy; The hidden supposition of
reality; The invisible psyche, or proportion-
istic difference overriding many claims::

Logic of Tumors - Amongst a number of
extreme examples that provide a platform
for psychological learning, one is the logic
of tumors; A difference can be drawn between a physical and a mental barrier, producing many subtle or ambiguous cases;
Perhaps the patient most learns by con-
ceiving that a physical barrier is already
present; Or, conversely, it may be useful to
relieve a mental conflict that is producing

130

such a difficult, perhaps artificial distinction; In any case, the technique is to attempt to allow the patient to associate
freely between areas of the mind that may
have 'blocked passages'; Free-associating
is the basic platform, followed by encour-
aging a willingness to explore a more complete personality; A patient may resent
this, because the part of the brain that is
not being active represents to them another person, perhaps someone they feel
they know well; But it suits therapeutic purposes to connote to the patient that the
areas are really divided, unrealized aspects of their self; What they envy in other
people is really some aspect of themselves that has not been cultivated; This is
why fully developed people are not envi-
ous of each other; Stating this explicitly to
the patient may queue the proper mental
alignment to begin seeing afresh; And the
result may often be greater happiness, and
a greater readiness to relax::

Love - is an important measure of functionality, ranging from degrees of nepotism
to fully empathic bonds with others; Intellectual integrity is sometimes a function of
self-love, while at other times it may reflect
a stoic commitment to the larger society; In
either case there is a recurrent encounter
with a personal concept of the good, which
may easily refract negatively when the
specific needs of others are put on the ta-
ble; So there is a strong difference be-

131

tween functional love and notional love which may even exist at the level of government; Still, one should question a love that becomes unthinking; More often than not, it has stopped giving its gifts; Sometimes, imagination may be the most viable substitute when love cannot be found; If love is known as a contract of imagination, a contract of giving, or a contract of empathy, then it seems obvious that it should be known rationally to be a contract; When it is not known to be a contract rationally, there is a risk that knowledge of love is irrational::

===============M===============

Madness - Much thought depends on the view that madness is not an art form, which is after all irrefutable; But we should not go one step further and say that it does not *concern* art; Madness serves to benefit from an artistic relationship to life: something so flexible, that almost anything goes; Indeed, if mad men were judged contextually to be artists exclusively, I predict that many of the mentally ill would be happily adapted within those constraints, provided there was no means to harm themselves; Art, without constraints, is the natural medium of the mad man, who can thereby satisfy his subtle yet perhaps superficial---although demanding---neediness; Beyond food and drink and all possible emotional benefit, art could serve to circumvent the irrational demands of the mind, and provide reassurance of permanent effectiveness on earth; But, mad men are often frustrated by physical materials, which restrict the subtlety of their minds; Therefore there is a great opportunity to employ the mentally ill in mental apparatuses (computers, non-invasively), particularly if it is determined that there is something useful to do with their work, as this would promote their sense of willfulness and self-desert.

133

Marshaled Senses - are a common refer-
ent point for some speakers about rationality and the value of reason; Some argue
that the senses should be marshaled in
order to stimulate reason; Others feel that
'marshaling' is itself a source of weakness,
by creating an embattled mind, or an unnecessary conflict with nature; In this second sense, 'marshaling' may be an over-
used military metaphor, that cannot stand
in for the 'real realities' of our senses;
However, in this sense, could the senses
be 'genetic', could they be 'typical'?, could
they be 'believed'?; The view seems to accept an excessively normative concept of
what the senses are, a passive role that
does not accommodate 'mind building' or
'reformative health'; Nonetheless, what if
someone is without mental control?; Does
the mere concept designate something
positive between pure function and pure
dysfunction?; A psychologist may argue
that these are ideals, and after all many
patients seem to have intuitions which
benefit from structured thinking; So no
more complex thesis is necessary; After
all, specific structures of thought are
largely determined by the individual or individual circumstance.

Maslow's Hierarchy of Needs - could be
modified if there were a higher paradigm
than function; One possibility for adding
dimension to the hierarchy is to include

significance in a duality with function; Another prospect is modularizing functionality
in a manner that renders it typologically
quantifiable; If there were multiple categories of functionality or multiple variables
which constitute a holistic functional category, we could ascribe them here; Here we
see the value of generic classifications---
the way 'dream' connotes sleep, and the
way 'food' does not include gluttony---
Surely this pyramid is as solid and dead-
ended as Aristotle's Categories---useful,
but only just; It begins to look valuable to
pursue significance by itself, and leave
health as a valuable after-thought; Otherwise, what is the use? Not everyone
should be a body-builder---such a thing
could strain the mind.

Meaningful Praxis -

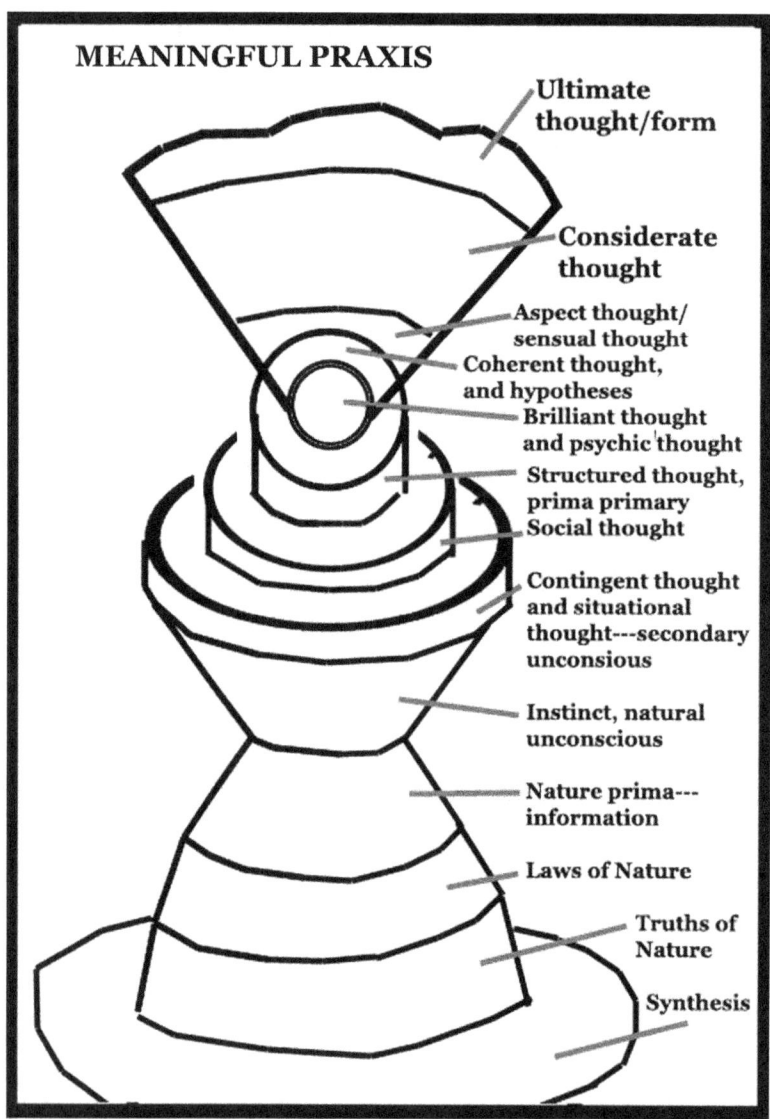

MEANINGFUL PRAXIS

Ultimate thought/form

Considerate thought

Aspect thought/ sensual thought

Coherent thought, and hypotheses

Brilliant thought and psychic thought

Structured thought, prima primary

Social thought

Contingent thought and situational thought---secondary unconsious

Instinct, natural unconscious

Nature prima--- information

Laws of Nature

Truths of Nature

Synthesis

::

Memory and Insanity - One of the things standing in the way of a pure brain model of psychiatry is the adaptive dependence of mental phenomena on multiple regions of the brain; In other words, functionality is sometimes more mental than physical; One theory that supports this is the connection between memory and insanity, specifically theories involving the availability of memorable words; The words seem to become available when they are most desired, but without full mental function, the mind is more likely to invent new significances; Even without a high IQ some of those secondary words may seem preferable, but the most important condition for finding *exactly the right word* is a purely mental state; It is neither precisely desire, health, or IQ that contributes, but something more like 'the ability to ideally associate'; If it is ignored what quality of word is being searched---that is, if the task is purely a function of the individual's perceived utility for the word---the result is a search that is not a function of IQ, but rather some other form of functioning; Insanity, however, affects the availability of the choicest words.

Mental Handicap -

what forces a mental handicap?

perfect-ionism	object-ivity
logical degener-ation	no way out

Although the theory that mental handicaps are caused by a reasonable process is widely rejected, a rational method is actually required for a respectable irrational theory of the same; There are four respective theories in general, two of which (A and C) I reject as over-simplistic: (A) Rational rationalism is the view that mentalities are justified by the mind; This is generally refuted by material specifics, e.g. determinism; (B) Irrational rationalism, is the theory that some minds can be rational in irrational ways; Largely this becomes a domain of extreme rationalism, and thus does not apply to the handicapped case; (C) Irrational irrationalism generally lacks a standard for argument; In complex cases it can be designated as the theory in which contexts are justified by an exterior means; This is not very helpful for the case of the handicapped, although it does explain some forms of unexceptional intelligence; (D) Rational irrationalism is the assumption that unexplainable things can be explained through reason, and also the dependence on reason in formulating a thesis about dysfunctional intelligence; This is the option I considered in formulating the above diagram;

Considering the diagram again, the reversal of the four quadrants yields four prospective methods leading away from handicap; The terrain is deceptive:

Ways out of handicap:

1. Lack of objectivity;
2. Lack of perfectionism;
3. Lack of degeneration;
4. Opportunity;

It is the final two options which must be focused on if someone is to find the slightest evidence of progress beyond a very limited condition of intelligence; The difference between the debilitation of the schizophrenic and the debilitation of the mentally retarded is that the schizophrenic is capable of making a self-guided journey, a series of 'instant evidences' for progress, whereas the mentally handicapped must rely on exterior forces for guidance; If there is a link between mental retardation and another disorder, the difference sometimes lies in the exteriorization of the guid-

ing object; The distance between the individual and his or her goals can create the
appearance of stupidity, in the same way a
schizophrenic is held back by interior conflict::

Mentation (Thought)- In a loose theory,
may consist of four types, each with four
stages; See the following diagrams, which
read counter-clockwise from upper right:

BASIC MENTATION

OCCUP-IED	DISTR-ACTED
COMP-ELLED	OPEN

LOWER INTERMEDIATE
MENTATION

CALM	DELIB-ERATE
PENSIVE	REST-LESS

→

HIGHER INTERMEDIATE
MENTATION

ORIENT-ED	OBSESS-IVE
SING-ULAR	RELENT-LESS

→

ADVANCED MENTATION

PARAG-ONIC	FOUND-ATION-AL
ELAB-ORATE	PER-FECT

::

Metanoia (and Metanoids) -

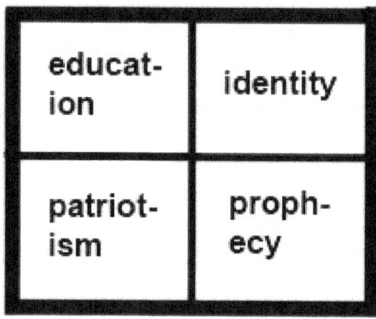

educat-ion	identity
patriot-ism	proph-ecy

Metanoia is a function of paranoia; It is forms of paranoia which have integrated with functionality; Once concepts such as identity and nationalism become interdependent with fear, even for purposes as benign as inspiration, motivation, or conservation, the nature of paranoia becomes inbred as a mimetic reference; This is not to say that fear manifests as a symptom in conscious terms, but rather that the significance of these general concepts is interrelated with the significance of fear; This may be in a form which is not oppressive except when individuals feel feelings of fear; Thus, as a paradigm it supports the common belief---whether it is gradual ore residual---in survival of the fittest; The breadth of the four metanoid concepts illustrates the profound effect fear or even madness may have upon society, culture, and psychology; Here are the reasons for the four choices:

Identity: conformity vs. ambition;
Education: reward vs. punishment;
Patriotism: strength vs. weakness;
Prophecy: certainty vs. unknowns;

Although it is possible that these four concepts are foundational for the very existence of paranoia, I will prefer to believe
that these concepts are a function of the
more basic type of fear, which I interpret
as being part-and-parcel of what has become the paranoid complex, whether it is
linguistic, chemical, or merely a norm of
society;

Clearly enough the roles of intellectual figures in defining the importance of 'mere
words' such as identity may be an influence in the epistemological logic---what
some have called '*epistemolological*'---
which under-rides the existential frame of
reference for logical versus illogical
choices; The results are profound when it
is considered that the existential actor may
be comparing general concepts, including
metanoids, with specific concepts which
figure into multiple overlaps of the above
analogs, e.g. 'strength is punishment but
serves patriotism' or 'weakness seems
certain so it is a better prophecy' or
'ambition requires self-sacrifice which is a
form of punishment, but conformity instead
has no reward' etc. In the context of paranoia the existential actor may be forced to
expect irrational rewards instead of taking

143

risks which compromise the generalistic metanoids::

Metem Psychic - A stage beyond which the psyche becomes concerned with dynamic symbols and realities; It is a frequent allegory of childbirth, the transient temporal mastery which renders successions of mysteries and embodiments of thought, as though cut from whole cloth; However, the metem psychic doesn't only occur with childbirth; It occurs beyond a certain degree of social plateauing, and especially even outside of these instances, with people who readily engage intellect as a habit of daily life; These people may be especially clever, verbose, or perceptive, and find a mirror for their mental habits in the whims of daily life; By the time this ability is realized it is often unexceptional by terms of the life that has been lived; In other words, the ability itself is often ignored as unexceptional; Because of its role in daily life, the metem psychic is associated with synchronicity and serendipity, especially good fortune or happenstance, and thus can be affiliated with the feminine and universities or places of culture, where occasions of intellect are most likely to have merit; However, traditionally, the metem psychic is a humbler virtue which belongs to simple people outside of the universities; Thus, it may have a connotation of lower classes such as gypsies, and thus is not political as much as proverbial::

The "Method Method" (Personalities and Development) -

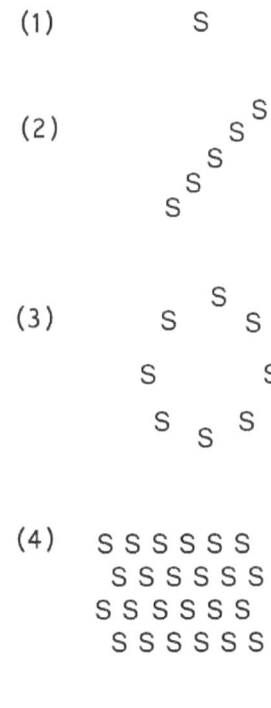

(1)

(2)

(3)

(4)

1. The qualities of the identical unit are exemplified. The good qualities of an appropriate entity are imitated. This may include the soul and government as in Plato's Republic, or healthy living as in Maslow's achievement pyramid, etc. Qualities may include sufficiency, functionality, empathy, wisdom, etc. Here the deductive method is merely repetition or resemblance, which has little risk of being subjective without poor reasoning. This entire stage is represented by the Amalgam. 2. Qualities of delineation and transformation are exemplified. These may be qualities of individuals who have gone through similar experiences, or else general qualities associated

145

with continuity, infinity, existence, perspective, etc. These qualities may include predictability, memory, excitement, self-sufficiency, etc. Here the deductive method is to find patterns which are most continuous, as represented by the Unitarian. 3. Qualities of coherence and pattern-forming are exemplified, as these qualities are best accepted by the individual. These may be social qualities of belonging, contributing, and succeeding, on the one hand, and qualities of comprehending, interpreting, and symbolizing, on the other. As a method of deduction it involves integrating, as represented by the Integrator. 4. Qualities of universalism and popularity are exemplified, as expressed by Kant's imperative and the choice between good and evil. This involves qualities of the world, nature, 'crowds', and conflicting points of view. It also may include solitude, resourcefulness, fortitude, and principle. As a method of deduction, it is a question of what is actually good---something but not everything.

The entire method is called the 'method method' because the same technique of repeating a symbol can be used in other typologies with a similar effect, e.g. by replacing unit, line, circle, and cluster with some other hierarchy::

Miasmos, The - A general symbol for complexity of perceptions, implicating the role of rational processes and the pull of the irrational drive; The miasmos plays a rational role in dream state, and an irrational role in waking life, implicating a duality, and suggesting that it may be seen as the 'passive double'; The miasmos plays an interesting role in relation to concepts of complexity, such as intellectualism, urbanism, and drama, typically by the use of surface references to the miasmos itself--- e.g. signs that the concept has been present in thinking---or a similar concept such as chaos, indeterminism, confusion, ambiguity, or arbitration; Emotional approaches to the miasmos, e.g. 'abandoned', 'weird', 'helpless' are often less structured, and thus can cause disorganization; But these cases frequently overlap with genuine emotional distress::

Mode Pathology - is a dimensional interpretation of some aspects of functionalism affiliated with a "top-down" approach; Patients may describe that something is going wrong functionally in their lives---that there is a 'mode inhibitor'; If there is not a mode inhibitor, it can be assumed that something is wrong with the patients themselves, when conflicts arise; Another option is when it is discovered that the patient 'has no problem'; Perhaps intellectual or emotional confusions were all that denied clarity; But this assumes a large de-

147

gree of function; Tentatively, the scenario might be further mapped in terms of unknown or ignored challenges, but studies have found that knowledge of these dilemmas is not always helpful; Instead of focusing on hardship or dis-knowledge, it may be beneficial to focus on either mode or perspective; The mode of the individual can be opaque or translucent, suggesting various answers in the context of the preceding critique; Someone may be closed/opaque and competent at working out a problem, in which case the only failure of therapy is the range and quality of resources provided for self-development, or otherwise the client may be dysfunctionally closed/opaque suggesting a prior failure of resources or guidance, and greater emergency; In the best case, closed dysfunction can be resolved by a few guiding words or an aphorism; Some patients appreciate receiving materials they can hold which provide 'material guidance' (however, it is important that this material has some specific relationship to the individual, either intellectually or pedagogically); Functional openness is often seen to be the most functional form of personality, but still might be watched for mistaken choices which could misinform an active personality, creating false commitments (see Sacrificial Dilemma); In the case of a functionally opaque appearance, it is clear that the client has some resourcefulness or is being manipulated; Sometimes a conversation about manipulation will make the client's motivations more clear; Efforts should be made to interpret how the individual is utilizing his or her inner resources, to show that a functional exterior means a functional interior; In the worst cases, functionality is a short-term commitment orchestrated to get some undesirable advantage; In this case, the personality may later degenerate to show compensation for disingenuousness; The danger with both types of functional personalities is the wrong type of commitment::

Modes of Approach - These vary in their simplicity and complexity;

reprehension
comprehension
retrospection
co-election
pre-descension

**A handful of modes
of approach**

::

Money - may be an important influence in the dimensionality of psychology; Wealth encourages synergistic combinations of quality and quantity thinking, most com-

149

monly propogated as the 'life planning syndrome' and less commonly as genuine life-philosophy; In-between it is possible there is some comparability to literal technical's, modularity, and process organization, all important qualities for positive dimensional psychology::

Mood Kinesthetic - The chemical contingency of what we call reality; The way we are naturally grouped by experiences, inclinations, and even intentions; Secondly, the organization of delineated existence into categories of perception, suggesting laws of travel or permeability; Thirdly, the dominance of a well-established mode of thought or feeling, producing a weakness to powerful, potentially ungrounded thoughts that relate with norms and conventions; Fourthly, the secret, psychic level of fully formulated thoughts and perceptions; In reverse order these correspond with the psychological correspondence with objects, producing an objective psychological hierarchy which scales to intelligence more than morality or sentimentality, except through specialized modes such as dreams or arguments; Thus, implicitly, the emotional is concerned with "imputations" of *any* level, whereas morality relates to specific constructions of correspondence *between levels* which pertain to this::

Moral Atavism - is to be distinguished from aesthetic concepts of atavism I introduce in later encyclopedias; While moral atavism is on the one hand a highly abstract concept, on the other hand it often bears association with distinctly real manifestations in society; Aspects such as illicit drug use and gambling are frequently cited as signs of moral atavism; But I mean to introduce it in a more positive light; Concepts as subtle as the flavor of tea are subject to moral atavism; The evidence is that words often degenerate; This occurs even for negative characteristics; For example, what was once called 'affront' is now called 'offense' or merely 'insult'; While these new phrases have conceptual importance, sometimes the usefulness is merely rational, and connotations are lost; The source of words in their origin is often to have a 'life of reference' and not merely 'ticketed meaning'; The major exception to the degeneration of negative words then, is merely the degeneration of references, which by and large may be considered an arbitrary construct, with concrete rather than conceptual verity; (Note that the common stipulation for the revision of such words is for a new conceptual significance, or 'objectivity'); The distinction is important; In the case of tea, someone may begin to say that what they expect is a 'smaller flavor' which has more to do with volume than with redolence; Words like melange have a subtlety which has become simplified into 'references' to flavors,

151

volumes, and exercises; But if no new exercise is introduced, if people are caught in a suspended significance, the only claim is to turn to old meanings for the required subtlety; The twin conflict at this point is the willingness to over-simplify and the basic inaccessibility of the social 'exercises'; These things (perspectives) should not be delusions in any sense, yet they do not always bear seriousness; The importance for moral atavism is that some values are trivial, whereas some obsessions are dangerous; And it is all the more difficult when some mere connotations of obsession are themselves trivial, creating false representations which masquerade as atavism, or, to perverted thinking, as values themselves; Although some principle is needed in generating social exercises, sometimes the idioms of the day do not even offer contingent significance; The good of the extrovert is as imperiled as the meaning of the introvert, although it is clear that that is where values are held::

Moral Fibre - Parents try to instill the essential moral teachings to their children; However, not all succeed in doing so; These may be very broad rules of emotional significance, and may depend on highly specific word patterns to succeed in use; Here is an example of a complete set:

Love is irrational:
you can't beg for love

Some geniuses lose their minds
The mind is sacred

It's important to have some
guiding principle;

Whether it is love
or knowledge, or practicality
everyone must know
or love, or be practiced
in something;

If you hold life's patterns
and objects to be sacred
like the mind,
life will reveal it's secrets to
       you;

Life isn't just you
And it isn't just other people;

You may try a wide variety
of things in life
but you don't have to like

all of them;

You can choose which
ones you like;

Some things are more
rewarding than others;

If one thing doesn't work,
You have got to try something
else;

There are some very important
people in life who thought
they were going to get every
          thing
and still aren't happy;

Happiness is a secret:

You can choose what secret
you want to work for you;
Happiness is one of the secrets,
But it's not the only one
If you want the world to love you,
You have to be reasonable

::
::

===============N===============

Narcotic Rules: (1) It shall not be pre-ferred where it re-frames life, except where life is disposable. (2) No risk shall be taken except where the drug does something unique to itself, and the potency can be resisted. (3) At long last, no preference shall be given to any individual drug, and drugs shall not replace ordinary food, unless they have the same value as food.

Nariety - [Nar-AY-eh-tee]; An isolated, in-formal, or contextually defined tick or neu-rosis; These may often be tacit, rational-ized exceptions to ordinary behavior; A nariety often registers as neurotic in the mind of the patient, but without a willing-ness to out-reason the effects of the nari-ety; This may mean that what is meant by 'informal' is 'casual' or 'permissible', but this raises the concern of potential gray areas as to when a neurosis becomes nearly a functional behavior; For example, what if such a nariety is an indicator of an otherwise latent un-diagnosed moral and behavioral problem? Whenever such a problem is serious, the nariety is apt to be interpreted as serious; In this sense, narie-ties may be manifestations of underlying guilt complexes; Then the question is raised what condition is absolutely nariety-free, if many social conditions are framed by the existence of a problem?; One the-ory is that functionality entails some de-gree of creative thinking to avoid narieties;

Another is that adequate coping with narieties involves a critical level of understanding such as empathy or contextualizing that entails adequate functioning; In this sense, a sensitive person may have a less serious nariety than someone who is comfortable with stiffness and unresponsiveness; Sensitivity becomes a psychological virtue, unless it is impulsive; Combining these two earlier theories, it can be understood that creativity is a kind of stress response---entailing sensitivity or a motivating condition----that may in some cases be more adequate than conventional functioning; Nonetheless, key aspects of human understanding such as empathy ease the difference between a rigid and an unconventional personality; The existence of sensitivity re-iterates that some narieties are not serious, whereas others are responses to stimuli that only appear when the individual is pathological; Such stimuli may include patterns of inward or outward dishonesty::

Nariety of Malapropism - Unlike it's more developed form, Acquisitive Language Disorder (Or-Gawp Disease), this nariety is characterized not by a set of assumptions or prevailing logic, but rather by a ready willingness to mask and avoid thoughts about functional language; The difference is something like the difference between schizoaffective disorder and paranoid schizophrenia, in that this form appears in quasi- or fully functional individuals but

may still have characteristics of mental im-
balance::

Natural Medicine (categorical approach) -

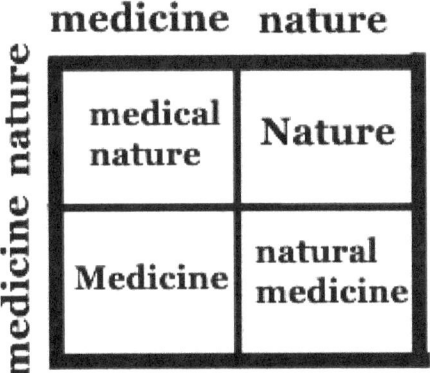

According to this view, homeopathy
(unlike traditional Chinese medicine) is
really inherently a view that the body can
stimulate itself, a denial that there is a real
medical problem in the first place; However, if it is admitted that the body has a
weakness, it may also be admitted that
there is a 'medical nature'; This does not
deny holism, only self-reliance;

Similar themes can be concocted
which claim that medicine denies the body,
but only if there is no body, or that nature
denies treatment, but only when treatment
is replaced by the function of nature;

It is only in this last step (category
four) that we reach natural medicine, as

essentially a relative definition of optimal treatment; For essentially, if nature were the natural path, life would be an indulgence; We would encounter no disasters;

Yet it is undeniable that, beginning with nature, natural medicine should be a principle that works for everyone in an ideal setting; This confirms my thesis that setting has more to do with treatment than is widely believed;

If life were cognitive enough that medicine influenced the luxury of location, then medicine should specifically target the portions of the brain which improve location; Such treatment could be general purpose, and early-acting::

Negative Ascription - Although already included in positive ascription according to connotation, negative ascription plays a special role in the lives of some patients; One initial understanding is that it is simply so embroiled in their personal lives that it cannot be translated without profound subjectivity that may be deemed either linguistically transparent or linguistically opaque; It is also possible that the patient is less obsessed with what is problematic about this behavior, leaving a sort of viable blindness; It may be said that professional negative ascriptions usually take place systematically, and therefore are prone to systemic failures; The other option is that the therapist has a literal bias or blindness about the circumstance or preferred perspective of the patient; However, within some acceptable arrangements, the patient's perspective may not always be infallible; The positive efficacy of advice is frequently reported, with some extreme exceptions, creating a kind of "therapist's gamble" when it comes to even the commonest wisdom; However, a patient's negative ascriptions fall within clearly individual or social vectors, creating a need to resolve personal or social direction; Personal negative ascription is often averted by 'focusing on the positive'; This can be effective whenever willful action could avoid harm, and may exist in degrees, which primarily has effect through perspective and belief; Social ascriptions which are negative may be difficult to change, but sometimes change can be created by suggesting individual action or creativity, or organization; Some people are capable of radical change through organizing, while others find that only subtle, creative differences have effect::

Negative Psychology -   A firm principle develops based on reverse psychology, that people, corporations, etc. are more committed to their negative than their positive. This is rooted in motivation. For example, the person who feels stupid is motivated to give the image of brilliance. The person who feels ugly is motivated to show off, etc. If it were not for these psychological principles, then we could say that

159

things are as they appear. But the same is true for psychology itself: what is truly psychological is in fact more-than-psychological. What is truly philosophical is more-or-less-than-philosophical. Because, as a rule, those who succeed are either motivated to compete against the traditions of the system, have things to learn from the system, or are complacent to the system and will not bring any effect upon the system. Thus, in one sense, negative psychology is true psychology, while in another sense, it has never been related to what psychology is.

Nepotistical Perception - It is interesting to note that there is a peculiar state of affairs which occurs for those (people, or animals), which are, like infants or conversely parasites within a host, bound to a particular state of affairs. This state is not much different from tunnel vision, and I equate it with the nepotistical. Nepotism, which I define as an obsession with cuteness, or by extension the obsession with the value of small things, is a state of affairs in which the thing nearest one gains a great importance, and outside things are judged in terms of a relation with that thing. This occurs for example, with the infant at the nipple, which is contrasted with the vision the infant has when viewing their mother (e.g. the viewing is great, whereas suckling is nepotistical). It is not that there is anything inherently wrong with nepotism. It is a form of adaptation which serves certain short-term advantages for the organism. An analogy can be drawn to functionality in general, that nepotism serves as a position from which the focus of functionality is narrow, and the emphasis is often on long-term survival. In this sense, its psychological function is one of security, and perhaps strategizing, or opening the channels of perception.

Noiac Studies or perception studies - May be approached when there are distinct levels of perceptions, producing degrees of difference (as opposed to categorical similarity or equivalence); These levels may be had for example, by comparing two complex negative concepts, such as alarm and danger, destruction and anger, or fear and monstrance; Here is given levels of perception based on alarm and danger:

APPREHENSION
ERRATICISM
LINGUALISM
FANATICISM

One may ask questions like, which is more extreme? Is there justified irrationality? Here is the same technique used in the case of destruction and anger:

| NEUROTICISM |
| ARROUSAL |
| STRIKING OUT |
| REVERBERATION |

One may ask for example, where is a patient most conscious? What is the patient willing to change? What would be most reasonable? Here is the same case given for fear such as paranoia and monstrance ('a source of fear'):

| REAL ASSOCIATION |
| MAL-IDENTIFYING |
| INTERNALIZING |
| EXTERNALIZING |

It can be traced for example, that all fears depend on some example from reality, but that the realization depends mostly on internal consequence. The decision then is, is this contrast chemically biased, or is there some way to transform the interior state? Further, there may be a form of subjective magnification that is happening as a result of the contrast between internal and external states. Exceptions may be remarkable.

Noir Sans - ("without night") - The often dramatized subject of a patient's impression of hospitals, and in particular, mental asylums; It may have roots in infantile memory, and then is sometimes recorded as a patient's final experience, a sensation of 'a bright light at the end of a tunnel'; To study these effects one need not look to hospices or the belief in infantile memory;

163

Afterall, many experiences are defined during the
period called adolescence; Many, including the mentally ill, enter a hospital in a state of fear; And young
mothers particularly record how at a particular point
the hospital seemed to want to take away their child;
The 'collective memory' of hospital categories is
compounded with the 'existentia' of whatever details
the patient ascribes to the hospital's negativity; However, as hospital environments improve, more often
some aspect of the hospital seems supportive or
even alluring; A small fantasy about working as a
doctor or marrying one may become a disillusioned
illness followed by a sentient interest in the experience of hospitals; Encouraged by video and computer games, individuals, particularly males, find a
duplicitous urge to believe that hospitals are homes
to monsters, and that they simultaneously fulfill fantasies; While a woman may fantasize about doctors
and abhor child birth, a man may find that hospitals
fall short of their private hyped-up video game mentality; Noir sans---which can almost be called a state
of being---seems to set a multiple standard upon
hospitals, first a minimal standard for psychological
appeal (positive, interesting, passable), and secondly
as a function of its necessity, even to fulfill life-
categories or serve as a mental apparatus; As hospitals become more and more a part of people's lives,
and a wider and wider range of personal characteristics become arbitrated by medical standards (I cite
the upcoming "heyday of genetics" cited in popular
magazines), it is incumbent upon us to parse this
quality of Noir Sans, in its many affecting details
upon the public consciousness; While requirements
for hospitals may seem expensive or complex from a
procedural point of view, many hospitals already
have a standard of activities for patients and also

use a wide variety of technologies; These
two characteristics suggest that
'programmatic impressions' are already
part of a working system, and additional
such measures could easily be implemented; Perhaps if a hospital has to be a
nightmare, there is something to learn
from the movies, or other media; The primary stipulation is that hospitals are not
just 'one category', and fulfilling multiple
functions means multiple psychiatric
benchmarks::

**Non-Statements - Negative Space and
Negation - Affirming Evidence -** These
are components traditionally grouped under the classification 'nonsense' and may
consist of dream imagery that plays a simple reassuring role, or waking fantasies
which may have intended value, but do no
always bear out; In the case of dreams,
usually obvious but difficult-to-explain images, such as occur in lucid dreams;
These may be products of active intelligence rather than an unconscious drive;
Non-statements play an important role in
defining the negative space, and the system of individual rewards (both simple and
arbitrary rewards found in daily life); Statements which are otherwise meaningless
may hint to the client's hidden desires or
auspicious awakenings; Although the
awakening may be done-in by morbidity, at
every stage of life there are potential
egresses upon the palatable value and re-
form possible by dealing directly with the

imagination; If there is an immediate negative aspect it is the person's willingness to second-guess (the long-term negative aspect is morbidity or bitterness, which may taste sweet); In general, youth and adults are encouraged by a variety of the same signs; One should not obsess over the complexity of affirming previous contexts of reference; Instead, similar combinations of visual stimulation, basic values such as moral fibre, empathy about desires, and general identification should be used; Late in life it may be important to combine more than one technique to give a sense of accomplishment, or to encourage free-association; All people have some amount of psychic power, whether or not it manifests in a form that can be semantically verified; Therefore, the associations developed later in life are actually the implicit context for previous frames of reference; Essentially, people grow and develop to suit the size and quality of their context, no matter if the context is suited to short-term or to long-term intuition; The tendency towards requiring long-term intuition is essentially a product of limitations upon quality of life; Eliminating dangers, nourishing the mind and body, and providing visionary signs contribute to a better sense of negative space, not merely as a phobious danger, but as a thriving fantasy with the power to affirm beliefs and channel energy.

Objective Structures - This may be seen as relating fundamentally with the character of what it is to have a stable versus an unstable mind; The following quadra may be seen as related to 'found psychology' on multiple levels (see also the "Method Method" and appendix labeled Development Hierarchy for further ideas):

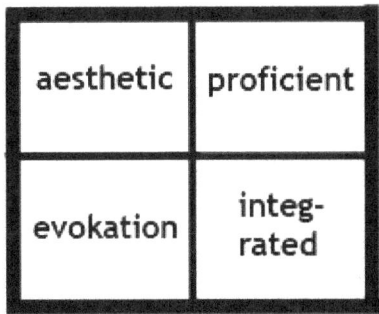

Proficient structures are those produced by desire and preferences; They are the 'effective' outward character of objects, often a reflection of the strength of the individual mind; (It cannot be said that a strong mind cannot 'ad-equate' experience); Aesthetic structures are a function of the faculty of judgment, and correspond to the location and appropriateness of experience; If this component is relative, it may also be absolute; Evocative structures are one degree more objective, and may carry a hidden message, which is some-

times more functional than the mind; Evocation is the source of madness in the
schizophrenic and demented mind, but is
the source of truth in the functional mind;
Evocation corresponds to emotional truths
and the durable qualities of *mental* experience; These aspects may be considered
justified by aesthetic judgments, of any degree of objectivity, and there is some evidence that they may exist independent of
any type of proficiency, although what this
suggests is not always a 'fair game'; Integrated structures refers to the justice of the
mind within experience, and universal
judgment; Hence it is legitimate to relate
with temporal versus atemporal states; Reality is only distorted by real things, and
the emphasis should be on disposable versus supportive realistics;

Interpreting the original diagram there is a
further level translating the first:

perfect-ion	compl-exity
select-ive perc-eption	symbol-ism

Preferences encounter the dimension of
complexity, aesthetic encounters perfec-

tion, evocation encounters selection, and integration encounters symbolism; The result is reductive, but complex, a form of radical contingency; The following diagram expresses the relationship of the parts (it can be seen that complexity and perfection synergize selection and symbolism):

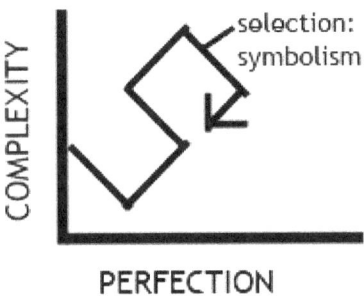

PERFECTION

The clear result is a concept of objective structures::

The Objective View of the Mind -
(Investigating or instigating the mind): This is a view in which the mind has more than a functionalist purpose; At the very least, a great intelligence or motivation could be ascribed to the way the mind composes itself, and the range of daily interactions which could be considered meaningful; One approach to this is that the mind has an industrial relationship to experience, that it serves as a 'forge' for archetypes it may itself find; Perhaps this view is ultimately a behavioral one, in which func-

tional relationships form the basis for what one later considered archetypes; In this sense, the correspondence between mind and archetype is no more than diagram-matical; But this betrays the purpose of psychology; Afterall, isn't it impossible to have an objective view of people that can be so much abbreviated? Either such dia-grams are themselves representations of individuals, or something has been missed, some more innate, arcane propin-quity of the mind; Perhaps the mind is not so much a forge as an observer upon some form of 'theatrical production'; But this is too diagurgical to believe; It has made too many moves; We do not rely on life to determine every function outwardly from the individual; Such a view is almost anti-psychological; So that nature of mind is in some way original, yet in some way that may be similar to this, it is also func-tional; Where the behaviorist is forced to believe that the individual is a devil, and the dramaturge is forced to believe that there is a devil behind the scenes, the originalist merely concludes that function and origin have vast similarities::

Sometimes an **Odd Vote** or suggestive-ness may be the only influence affecting a course of action; This raises dangers of neurotic and psychotic behaviors; Some would say that this 'voting' is best vetted by a level of adequate screening, e.g. a mental process or behavioral distraction that is more functional or normal than a suggestion; However, this produces a certain implacability; In other cases, even normal development may go so far as to have 'theories' of adequate response; In this case, the function of suggestion must be seen to rely on the theories, suggesting that the theories must be highly functional::

Oedipus Complex -

Alternatives to the Oedipus Complex

Greed of Suspection: As a general theory of human evil, it may do well to mention how underrated sheer imagination and superstition have been; Not everyone has the rational mind of a psychologist; Indeed, the development of 'crazy' or ersatz theories is widely reported to contribute to the tendency to violent acts in some individuals, although the two things may be chemically unrelated; I will treat environmental factors as separate from the case of genuine suspicion, if it is recognized that paranoia, whether it is a mere quality or an entire state of mind, cannot be both exponential and relative without seeming endemic; So the case is one of suspicious properties which I suggest are not ever themselves paranoid, but which are doubtless contributors to paranoid symptology; It is in this objective sense that I search still further, finding evidence that, if paranoia is not its own quality, then surely there are

171

rational groundworks for paranoia considered exclusively as a form of perception; In
that case, the 'Oedipus complex' (the case
of the conditions called by that name) is
not as much a latitude of desire as it is a
hazarding of guesses or 'feelers' which are
only determined if they are determined absolutely; Then it is possible to study the
root condition as contingencies rather than
convictions or opinions; This opens the
way to consider that there may be complex
physical (conditional or exceptional) explanations which open the original problem
set to other broader and less determined
explanations::

Orbits / Orbit Theory: Accepts the spe-
ciezation of semen as a foundation for understanding that men in particular have a
metaphysical reliance on benignly targeting their fathers, e.g. instead of reacting
against ejaculation emotionally, they respond to birth and development by main-
taining a dependence on the physical act
which has already occurred; This is not
always linguistically developed, as not all
males are linguistically developed; But
when there is any such corresponding development, there is also a corresponding
passive targeting of the father; The absence of physical attraction in the memetic
sense---that is, flesh on flesh---can be understood as an aversion to the surprising
equivalent scale of the father---e.g. if the
father were one hundred feet tall, there
would be an urge to repeat the semen

172

journey by rubbing the penis on the giant's ankles (almost asexually); This aversion to the father is also explained by abstraction of reference; Of course, the abverse happens in females in a manner that may be more complex: the daughter tries to draw her mother to her because her mother represents her closeness to birth and orgasm; In related ways, the daughter may draw the father near to attract the mother, and the son may draw the mother near to attract the father, playing roles that are both neutral and meaningful for mental process (contrary to Freud); Although these impulses may seem secondary, they are actually primary if subtle motivators: e.g. because the identical sex represents sexual functionality---the tree of life or cosmic egg or similar iconizations::

Optimal Behavior -

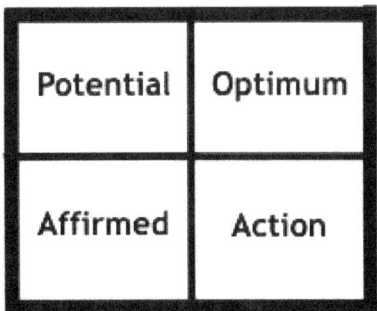

Potential	Optimum
Affirmed	Action

The denial of one of these factors, such as the optimal, potentials, affirmations, or actions, reduces the amount of optimal behavior::

Optimal Personalities - I have discovered three types of optimal personalities:

1. Socialite Type: most successful type
   Description:
   > Symbol of self-
   >> intelligence
   >
   > With language of political behavior
   > With system of social
   >> personality

2. Deliberating Type: Most Accomplished Type

   Description:
   > Symbol of political per-
   >> sonality
   >
   > With language of social
   >> intelligence
   >
   > With system of self-
   >> behavior

3. Ambitious Type: Most Creative Type

   Description:
   > Symbol of social behavior
   > With language of self-
   >> personality
   >
   > With system of political
   >> intelligence

Then these types propose a dilemma 'Independent of the types, which of the following is preferred?'

A. Life as work-of-art vs. superficiality
B. Pep vs. discouragement
C. Reachable goals versus
   blindness

By encountering blindness, discouragement, and superficiality (the three demons
of personality) there is great potential for
growth and learning; However, the appearance is one of art, pep, and reachable
goals::

Or-Gawp Disease, or Repetitive Acquisitive Language Disorder - is an underesti-
mated influence in developmental, social,
and psychotic thinking; Nonetheless sometimes it will not be diagnosable until after
treatment for a more aberrant problem; Yet
it occurs across disorders; It occurs when
old definitions or notably individual words
are used to explain new definitions and
contexts; Often there is some adaptivity,
e.g. an ability to change definitions gradually, but the difference between definitions
becomes fossilized as a set of prevailing
assumptions; It would do to be careful
about the uselessness of the disease,
since it also manifests at a higher level of
function in the form of the Nariety of Malapropism; The only difference may be cognitive function, suggesting that the disease
itself may exist in some form even for
highly adapted people::

175

=============P=================

A paradigm called the **Pace of Happiness**
goes a long way towards explaining subjective characteristics of psychology; One
might suspect that this view originates in a
kind of self-assured professionalism on the
part of the clinical therapist, rather than
psychological realities of the unconscious
or archetypal kind; However, if there are
choices made on the subject of psychol-
ogy---and who would accept a world without such choices (perhaps a robot)---
happiness is primal ground for defining the
function of such choices; The fundamental
concept becomes not one of reference
(static objectivity), or one of mere agreement such as correspondence, but instead
depends most fundamentally on the agent
of choice that makes the final determination about significance---whether it is significance carried over into other systems,
or instead translated into a surfacial---
incidental---mode of behavior; The clear
relationship here is between happiness---
that is, the functional state, which priori-
tizes movement---and the pace of life,
which is outwardly not inherently a correspondence between the self and other
agents, thus reflecting the capacity for a
'constant continuum' between the self and
nature; Happiness (whether or not it is
conscious in its aspect), becomes the req-
uisite not only for officiating perception,

such as thoughts that are memorable---
here adopting a relative standard---but
also for communication between people,
and perhaps symbols or memes; 'Chains
of happiness' become the standard for interpreting psychological causation, an effect which becomes suspiciously economi-
cal, political, or 'derogatory'; Yet it is certainly a positive impulse for the individual,
which clarifies the reasoning for the
causes and effects, much in the same way
as the Apercu::

Parable Psychology - Also called modular psychology (as distinct from parapsy-
chology for 'paranormal psychology') is the
dimension of psychology in which proto-
types or 'parables' of function are compared to ordinary or abnormal function, determining a form of 'dream function' or al-
tercation from a pre-determined view;
These altercations may take place as
though no decision occurred; Alternate
methods can be applied as a component
of the system, including comparative function involving multiple parables, coherent
function involving all related 'dream functions', or correlated function involving a
prescribed 'dream path'; If these seem like
forms of hypnotism, it can be cited that a
parable does not have an inherent chemistry; Instead, it scales to the more mundane
functions of daily life, in their level of function; Nonetheless, defined 'dream functions' have a potential to reinforce the

177

strongest personal motivations, and to inspire motivated work on the job and elsewhere; An involved sense of 'parable process' would investigate viable life categories, and expand them, treating them like
fantasies; The result often is to re-vitalize
dormant creativity and enforce rational impulsivity; For this purpose it may be a
prevalent response to a variety of mood
disorders, including major psychiatric disorders under treatment::

Parachyrae - (meaning semi-magical,
quasi-alchemy); An obscure subject, associated especially with alchemical concepts
of self-development, in particular, animal
forms and ratios of human form and their
manifestations in higher development;
There are at least three basic types: (1)
The lower animal, the man, and the higher
animal, (2) The half-man, the full-man, and
the double-man, and (3) The animal, the
man, and the half-man-half-animal; The
bodies of theory on the subject offer a difference between moral (1), immoral (2),
and amoral (3) development, with some
exceptions for very peculiar rules such as
magic, hermaphrodism, and paid enter-
tainment::

178

Paradigms in Therapy -

POND LOGICAL DIAGRAM OF PARADIGMS

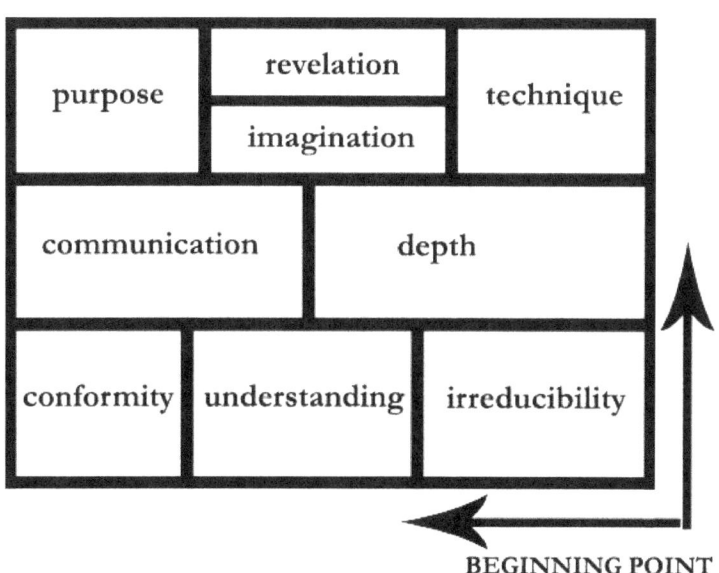

BEGINNING POINT

::

Paradoxical Judgment - A question arises: What is progress?

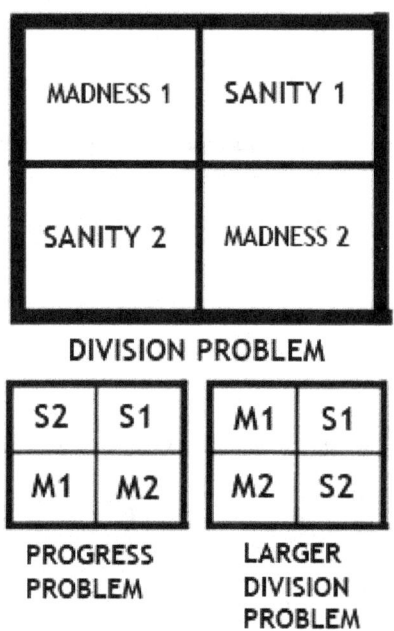

DIVISION PROBLEM

S2	S1
M1	M2

PROGRESS
PROBLEM

M1	S1
M2	S2

LARGER
DIVISION
PROBLEM

An infinite continuum of sanity[1], sanity[2], sanity(n) just looks like linear thinking, perhaps an insignificant expression of iterated enumerations;

We can propose [1] All valid worlds have valid formalities; or [2] Madness is not a continuum; Or, [3] Sanity may oppose itself, but otherwise we are likely to reach a problem such as:

180

[A] Sanity is incoherent, [B] Madness is sometimes a form of sanity, or [C] Madness is not the opposite of sanity::

Paradoxical Praxis - Relating to four types: Excited, Irrational, Bitter, and Depressed: In a constructive framework leads to mental types that are marginally more functional: Temperamental, Motivated, Egoistic, and Modulated; See the following diagram:

irrational	temperamental	excited
motivated	functional	modulated
bitter	egoistic	depressed

Each of these is a response to the conflicts native to their constituent areas (the earlier categories); The total sum of responses then amounts to a kind of paradoxical function; This does not work across axis diagonally without working across both diagonals; Thus, the depressed type may be modulated by the excited type, and have its ego supported by the bitter type, but ultimately the decision to be depressed is irrational, since it is neither egoistic nor modulated to be depressed; Thus, paradoxically, the choice *against* depression is also irrational, but supports ego and modulation; If all the choices are irrational, the depressed person would have nothing to do, but in fact, when there is some modulation and some ego, there is room to fight depression; It must be decided that these elements are not depressed, even when the choice seems irrational; For the irrational, the choice is essentially the opposite: they must choose to feel depressed about irrationalism; However, the diagram contains other messages as well: (1) The temperamental is not really bitter or depressed, and thus has an opportunity for positive irrational and excited choices, (2) The motivated is not really excited or depressed, and thus has an advantage in overcoming irrational and bitter choices, (3) The egoistic is not really irrational or excited, and thus has an advantage over bitterness and depression, and (4) The modulated is not really irrational or bitter, and thus defends against both excitement and depression; See also the Meaningful Praxis::

Paroxology - (paro-xos: to make sharper) is the study of development such as learning, emotions, or pathology in terms of available opposite concept pairs; Arguments can be made for example, on the basis of the correspondence between volition, inflection, personality, and affect in relation to assumed or construed systemic variables, which are in turn affiliated with the client's "concepts" such as word associations; A simple test can be performed such as by using the question "What words first come to mind"; If this proves inaccurate, profiles can be taken from subject categories, e.g. "What do you think of when I use the term 'happiness'"; This can be combined with Rorschach type results, and compared for contrast with interests the individual has declared, with current social symbols as a background; The goal is not so much to see what is normal about the patient, but rather to trace what *combinations* are most potent to the individual; For example, there may be a big difference between someone who does programming to raise a family, and someone who feels it is avant-garde; It may then be tested if programming means a family to both types, or if the basis for the interest is purely conceptual versus practical; If programming is a popular trend, the family answer suggests a popular concept of family, and the conceptual answer suggests a popular concept of concepts; If programming (or some other selected interest) is not a popular topic, one can fish for some further concept which indicates that the interest is popular for them individually, rather than socially; In this manner, there is a kind of criss-cross pattern which establishes that *some* set of opposites is the context for the patient's reason-

183

ing; Even if the mood is completely neutral, there may be some key concept which spurs emotions or neuroticism; But if that is not the case, it may be suggested that therapy is not making progress::

Paroxysm of Identity - is relatively what identity does; If it does not change, it must realize change; If it does not fixate on an idea, it thrives on a dynamic; Both dynamic and unchanging realizations are general forms of paroxysm; And it should not be assumed that these reactions are merely physical or merely behavioral; Indeed, paroxysm is too individualistic to be behavioral, and too existential to be physical; The effect of an incidental concept such as the literal 'paroxysm' is rightfully alienated from the idea that some similar effect could have an equivalent identity; But nonetheless, it has biological incident; As a function of thoughts, the body may sometimes thrive, as is reported in near-death events; And this is all the more true with functional thoughts---not always as a consequence of the functioning of the mind, but sometimes the language itself, as it is composed independently of experience; We should abandon the subjectivity that arbitrarily denies language, and at that point experience ought to be fully rectifiable; Such is the paroxysm, a form of rational abnegation of negativity; But we should not underestimate and say that this process is not itself a process, does not

184

itself consist of some identity and series of real events::

Penis Makers and Life Destroyers -
There are hidden races which are concealed beneath the exteriors of personalities; What are they? Perversity fetishes nested within recognizable, perhaps unavoidable types; Men have been characterized by women as 'erecting monumental erections' to glorify the phallus; If there is a trend against this, it is the idea that that organ is 'the thing to conceal' and that the desirable man is God not man, aspects which are certainly more conscious in the minds of women, sometimes because great men promote them, but more often because these beliefs seem to suit the nature of appearances; In some cases an irony develops born from an irrationality involved in the attraction to the male sex, thus creating a dual nature between the concealed and unconcealed penis; It might be said that the characteristic of duality permeates female relationships, and may only be exaggerated by this detail; Certainly the female fetish is the most obvious motivation for male egoism; But also dormant, or politically apparent, is the hunter instinct and the allegory that semen are 'feasters upon flesh'; The wish to dominate appearances may actually be secondary to the male wish to dominate unconscious forces, represented by the battle against mortality---a battle which to the woman's

185

ear seems ironic, mal-conceived, and self-ish; Yet this battle occurs in mortal terms; The woman overcomes this by giving birth, thus her perversity is not one of appearances, as in the penis fetish (and men resent her for denying this), but instead a mirthful question of honesty about life and death, a root which runs deep into virginity, abortion, and maternity; These symbols in turn relate to other categories, such as achievement, deception, and cruelty, which are sometimes governed by referring to male personalities, but otherwise may take place directly in the personality; The female type has great awareness, but also frequently a material fatalism; It is at this point that it is seen that females rely on tools more than men, reflected in a feigned dependency and belabored conquest of the male fetish::

Perception Studies - See Noiac Studies ::

Perduralism - The notion that ideas naturally age, so that ideas that once seemed irrational are now prospectively habitual; A distinction is made between moral or irrational perduralism, and ordinary or rational perduralism; Since some minds age ideas faster than others, it becomes possible to forgive someone on the basis of their natural thought patterns; It may also be possible to forgive the insane more than the sane::

Permiscu (Psychological Concept) - Named after 'permissivity' or 'promiscuity', is the psychological principle of 'going out on a limb'; It is not merely association or curiosity, but the mental desire for information; It is also the mental faculty of contextualizing understanding; It can be compared with the Apercu, so that, if we realize that the permiscu is always complex, then the context that is understood becomes complex unless the Apercu is simple; Thus, the figure of understanding reduces either to sheer complexity---both complex---or a figure of conceptualization in which 'permiscuous' exploration is a function of the state of mind; What this does not say is one of two things: (1) That complexity is unreasonable, and (2) That the state of the mind is a conceptualization; What the permiscu explores then is something like complexity and state of mind; If complexity reduces it is something like the this-ness of exploration, not an objective quality except by reference to the Apercu; But, however, if the Apercu is objective, then so too may be the permiscu; When the Apercu is simple, it is difficult to see how they might not both be understood, even if only situationally; Thus, the only barrier imposed to the psychology of realization is the individual person's frame of reference, when it is complex; See also the Apercu::

187

Perspective Pathology - Is a dimensional interpretation of some aspects of functionalism, affiliated with a "bottom-up" approach to pathology; In this view, in contrast to Mode Pathology, in which environmental factors or the internal are to blame, complete trust is given to the individual to develop according to what may be personal criteria; Thus it is important to discriminate precisely what seems viable to the individual, and also to reassure the patient that it is possible to change perspective without affecting the course of one's life; In this view, there is a duplicity between passive perspectivism, which can be accepted as necessary and inconsequential, and active perspectivism, which is by contrast unnecessary and entirely consequential; This dynamic is realized especially in the context of the status quo; After orienting the individual on these statuses, they may well decide they are creative decision makers with the power to orient their lives; Even if not, they may be open to input about how to be oriented, or what things about their lives may be relied on for structure and dependability; Individuals should be encouraged to plot out some structure on paper, or craft opinions about society, for when doing such things, one gains agency and consequentialism; If one has control, it can be wagered, then life is a creative dream boat and there is nothing stopping us from having that perspective as a conviction::

188

Perspective Psychology - Looking at an individual perception, such as an arching bird, there is nothing that says that the impression is not psychological: indeed, psychology depends on that condition; To deny this is to be obsessed with the abstract or material sciences which obscure the motivations of the authentic individual; Returning to the image of an arching bird, the impression is one of meaning, such as metaphor, mired or conversely enhanced by all the habits, thoughts, and obsessions of the individual person; When that impression is extended to include concepts of self, the meaning grows still more complex, as impressions come to reflect not only an exterior token significance, but instead a genuine correspondence to the realm of interior psychology; Thus, there can be an informative quality in which the outer world betrays the thoughts and emotions of real interior, that is, established, identities; Because of this, psychologists do not follow the philosophers in asking if the world is not real, for such impressions (when they occur, if they occur) are inevitably the result of genuine interior conditions of self; It may be withstood however, that there is no rule preventing the self from indulging what Freud calls 'the most outrageous fantasies' or the most superficial realities, a condition in which the exterior objects becomes alienated without critical understanding; Thus there is a kind of critical thesis, that insignificant insights

189

should be criticized, whereas significant meanings only deserve questioning or encouragement::

At the top of the list of curable illnesses is what might be called **Peter Rabbit Syndrome** - the attraction to the hypothesis that psychology itself is to blame; Like the rabbit from the story, the trend is to "return again and again to the garden": either the individual can be blamed for the harmful activity, or the individual has a total lack of control; (the converse theory, that psychology is only a benefit, suggests that psychology itself attracts this behavior; this is usually considered harmless); Incidentally, when there is a real lack of control, an actual illness may be to blame; Peter Rabbit Syndrome is sometimes confused or extended into a general love of hospitals, as an explanation for individual behavior; This may correspond with respective indicators of poverty, loveless-ness, or especially conscious malnourishment, suggesting again that the case is not an illness but rather a form of crude adaptation, unless there is a lack of volition; Exceptions are sometimes found in ersatz brain developments, but the real cause may be similar, unless there is mental illness or a physical problem::

Poodle Effect - This is something I have noticed that is very important, so I will mention it first.People are often set off course by the appearance of poodles! Seriously!They think their brain is composed like a poodle, and then they have to undo the effect!Until they learn to squash in these exaggerated 'puffs' of their brain, there is no hope of recovering mental function.This effect is even more extreme on the brain than the hyper-activity resulting from sugar, only the effect is opposite.Overcoming the poodle effect could almost be called the first stage towards mental functionality. But we should ultimately avoid expressions like 'ascendent brain' as these may have similar effects, albeit not as extreme as the poodle.I have cured at least one person's thoughtlessness by mentioning this problem!

Popular Qualifier - One should be warned that in many cases popularity is a poor qualifier; To use the most popular example, outwards success does not always connote happiness; And coffee may be popular, but caffeine, rather than pure enthusiasm, has much to do with it; One might even suspect that popularity tends to be bought, or conversely that it exists for numinous or sublime reasons that are inexplicable, such as the whims of a deity; Clearly several categories emerge in relation to popularity: It may be a function of enthusiasm, artificial influence, or some

191

kind of pre-existing strategy, such as natural evolution; Perhaps enthusiasm is generally the weakest expression, but this may not always be the case; Studies show that a 'strong force' of motivation can sometimes overrule patterns of assumptions that seem to give absolute evidence of a different outcome; While a mother's protective influence upon children may be evolved, it can mean the contingent difference between life or death for the child; The 'popularity factor' for the child is situational, not genetic, or at least not in the same set of genes, so it looks as if there are some (other) cases where a pre-existing strategy would benefit by emotional integration like the mother and child; If that is extended into a broad case, artificial motivators may then be assumed to be highly relative, when the result may be some 'special combination' of pre-set and emotional responses; Whatever the qualifier, the nature of popularity must be highly context-sensitive; In the case of a drug, if it is the significance of stimulation that matters more than the empirical properties of chemistry for instance, cases must emerge (in the future if not now) where chemistry is a function of situations rather than drugs; Perhaps this assumes too much interaction between chemistry and environment; But such a case could certainly seem optimal, if it did not pose difficulties, for paradigms like the popular qualifier; Similar work has been demonstrated in Szasz::

Positer Characteristics [non sic] -

There is a project (called Positer Characteristics) to set out what typological domains are concerned with psychology, and
to describe them in as reduced a way as
possible, so as to permit all-encompassing
understanding; These domains might be
*architecture, objects, wilderness, and life-
forms*; Each is granted three dimensions,
using a technique in which every three-
dimensional box has three obvious alternatives, represented by the neighboring
boxes; I will continue on to describe the
boxes and a number of interesting translations of the categorical relationships;

[TRANSLATION ZERO: *Categorical
Deductions*

CATEGORY 1: Architecture

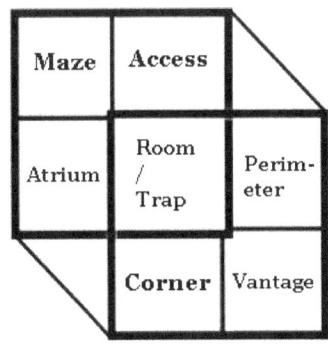

The room is a trap just as
the vantage is a maze
in the same way
the access is a corner just as
the atrium has a perimeter;

CATEGORY 2: Objects

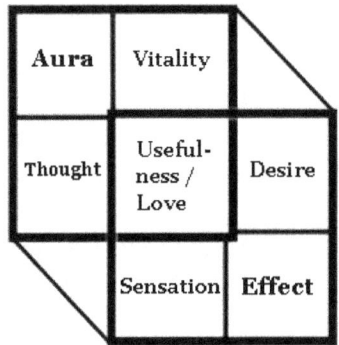

The love is useful just as
the aura has an effect
in the same way
vitality is a sensation just as
desire is the thought;

CATEGORY 3: Wilderness

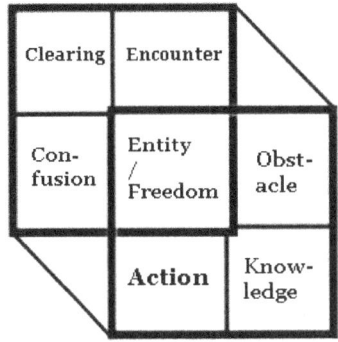

An entity is free just as
knowledge is clear
in the same way
an encounter is action just as
confusion is an obstacle;

CATEGORY 4: Life-Forms

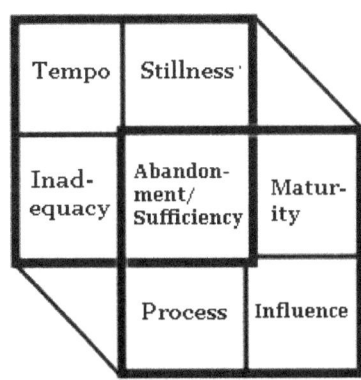

Abandonment is sufficient just as
there is influential tempo
in the same way
stillness is a process just as
inadequacy is mature;

195

---Continued subsequent pages---

By the end of this section, the goal of devoting the second book to three dimensions, where the first was devoted to two, is complete;

[positer characteristics, cont'd]

TRANSLATION ONE: *Four Categories*

Architecture of Objects

A room is love just as a trap is useful in the same way a maze is an effect just as a vantage has an aura when an access is sensation just as a corner is vital in the same way an atrium is desire just as a perimeter is thought;

Objects of the Wilderness

Love is an entity just as usefulness is free in the same way there is an aura of knowledge just as an effect of clearings when there is vital action just as an encountered sensation in the same way there is a desire for confusion just as there is a thought of obstacles;

The Wilderness of Living Forms

There is a sufficiency of entities just as a freedom to abandonment in the same way there is knowledge of tempo just as there is a clearing of influence when there is an encounter of process just as there is an action of stillness in the same way maturity may be confused just as the obstacle is inadequacy;

The Architecture of Living Forms

Abandonment is a trap just as sufficiency has a room in the same way influence is a maze just as tempo is a vantage when stillness is a corner just as process is an access in the same way inadequacy is a perimeter just as maturity is the atrium;

TRANSLATION TWO: *Two Categories*

The Architecture of Wilderness

A room is free just as a trap is an entity in the same way a vantage is a clearing just as a maze is knowledge when the access is action just as the corner is an encounter in the same way the atrium is an obstacle just as the perimeter is confusion;

The Objective Life-Form

Love is abandonment just as usefulness is sufficient in the same way an aura has in-

197

fluence just as the effect is a tempo when there is a vital process just as a sensation of stillness in the same way there is a desire for inadequacy just as a thought of maturity;

[positer characteristics, cont'd:]

TRANSLATION THREE: *One Category*

Objective Architecture in the Wilderness of Life-Forms

A room is free is an inadequate desire just as when a trap is an entity there is a thought of maturity in the same way a clear advantage is a vital process just as a maze of knowledge has a sensation of stillness when access to action has an aura of influence just as the encounter in the corner has the effect of tempo in the same way the atrium obstacle is a love for abandonment just as the confusing perimeter is sufficiently useful;

See also Psychological Location::

Positive Ascriptivism - takes place not only on a clinical level, but in the minds of those receiving care; Professionals are often warned about assumptions to that effect that a life might not be going well; Often only when every sign indicates functionality is the professional free to assess that that is the case; This sense of positive ascription carries warnings of its own, when it is possible that superficial signs are the only viable symbol, or when it is possible that patients are over-stretched merely to meet a fundamental requirement; Perhaps, for example, the individual is undergoing some kind of specialized recovery, as is common with poets and those who have had highly selective experiences; Indeed, some of these specialized approaches might be desirable; However, it is also possible that the patient is making positive ascriptions; First, it is possible to act outwardly and convert surface perspectives of other people into an assumption of self-effectualism (the patient does this); While this may be an effective platform for conformity, it is not always the best platform for genuine motivation; A second, more dangerous form of self-ascription is to project one's own qualities upon other people and events; This converts into an utter blindness of the real efficacy of those people and events, in a sense equitable with non-conformity and a selfishness illusion; Certainly if these people could be useful to society that selfish-

199

ness would appear inadequate; But that is not what science projects; Positive ascription in general might benefit from a mutual absorptiveness, which is one potential foundation for dynamic social functionality (See also Negative Ascriptivism)::

Post-Modalism (the contextual caveat) - Otto Rank and those after him sometimes wrote of a contextual psychology, sometimes based on emotionalism or compatibility between desire and conformity; These trends are not exactly socialist, indeed they are compatible with capitalism when there is growing room for shallow disillusionment; This 'science' as it might be called, accepts some degree of chemical arbitration, but sees the individual as the critical arbiter of experiences; Clearly, if the individual is not finding meaning, then there must be some relative purpose in this; There is a critical insight that history allows some pessimism for those that have an empathic vibe; But, being a vibrancy, it need not overwhelm; The usefulness of post-modalism, however, is not to second-guess the relationship between the psychic and conformity, but rather to reinstate the value of the individual---the situational significance---when it is realized that psychological systems are incongruous with identification, or when it is possible for individuals to have their own concepts of systems; I would like to express this as the belated intellectualization of individual therapy, which ironically is not post-modal at all, but affirms the modality of the individual; Finally, there is also an antithetical post-modalism (non-post-modalism) in which it is realized that it is psychology itself which has an intrinsic significance; This may be termed dimensional when the psychology is interpreted broadly to include the patient's concepts of significance; Perhaps it is the assumption that psychology is significant which people wished to overcome::

Pragmatic Assumption - In certain cases someone will be making a pragmatic assumption, such as in the case of 'In prior lives I must have been stupid, because I am not very brilliant now' or 'Art should be highly representational, because that is the form that best depicts reality'; While these statements are appealing as explanations of the world, and may be useful, in fact we should realize that in these cases it is the explanations which connote truth; In other words, if we could find another suitable explanation, this too could seem true and accurate; The pragmatic assumption is to assume that any explanation that seems adequate *is* adequate; If we shave off the layers of assumptions, what we are left with is essentially a self-generated explanation, which is subject to our own biases; This may be true in the specific context of language even in highly rational or 'objective' communications; Hence, psychology is useful in detecting exactly which things are true about our explanation; (1) It may be the explaining-ness of our statements about ourselves which connotes truth, which sometimes collapses to a mere emotional reality (however rational), and (2) Our self-explanation may intentionally deny truths which seem negative, which are undeniable actors within experience; Hence the pragmatic assumption may be dangerously defending a lie; The role of the psychologist is then to realize to what extent the patient is adapted to aesthetic or synthetic realities, because in the context of bias they connote reason; In other words, how flexible is the person's underlying balance of adaptability versus acceptability?; This may prove important::

Pre-Oralism - A concept experienced more amongst male patients than female, constituting a discomfort with food and a limited willingness to confront thoughts of penetration; This may be accompanied by limited social drive and a relatively suppressed sexuality; Patients may find this condition reinforces idealistic visions of life, or that it is merely an unwillingness to eat; In some cases this may be healthier than an eating disorder, and may be discussed as a way of raising conscience and tolerance of food::

Pre-Versalism - A rare innocent state in which an individual has good intentions without much evil influence, and may believe in accordance with his or her level of authority that the good intentions are adequate for a good life; If he or she does not feel authoritative, the view of the good life may be subverted with fantasies, or even a superficial 'supposition' of fantasy; The engenesis of a variety of guilt disorders can be originated in preversalism, even though preversalism does not connote guilt; The conclusion, then, is that guilt involves some identification with experience, such as a father or mother figure, or outside authority; This relates with the theory of guilt by authority::

Principal Development - The primary development of the individual, which corresponds to attitudes towards time, such as maturation, adaptivity, and perspective; The first stage (birth, childhood, and adolescence) roughly corresponds to priority commitments such as genetics, psyche, and volition; The second stage (adulthood) corresponds to late developments such as economics, ethics, and management; The third stage (age) corresponds to functional problems such as purpose, attachment, and validation; Through early incidence, there may be risks to health involving the 'inquisition' of the earlier priorities; Through life extension, there is an oppor-

203

tunity to re-introduce the earlier stages, with resulting benefits for life-structuring and health::

Prodigy - has a reputation for the paranormal; I don't mean UFOs or conspiracy theories, I mean that it is virtually definitive of normal behavior; Talented artists, original poets, and famous musicians all took their turn defining what it means to be "paranormal"; Resemblances of major works are now expected behaviors for students studying the rudiments of their disciplines; Also, greatness is often the standard by which daily activities are assessed and compared; Indeed, many people could be fooled into believing a talented actor is an 'ordinary person'; In light of this theory there is an obvious gestalt to apply, namely, 'Are prodigies the most functional citizens?' And many would say yes, but this brings a peril with bi-polar disorder, that ordinary actions should be assumed great only because they belong to them; While this may be well-trod territory emotionally, its 'incidental' significance, that is, intellectually, should not be considered contraband; Prodigy in a dimensional sense is not only functionality, but the inability to make assumptions; With this generalitic, there is a 'contingency to contingency' which should ideally (that is, conceptually) eliminate the parallel between symptoms and diagnosis in terms of intelligence; That is, unless a diagnosis represents a functional type::

Property Paradox - A particular conflict may arise between the interior and exterior identity; This occurs particularly between the anima and animus, representing the female and masculine parts of identity or consciousness; For example, the female may relativize her physical relation to males by having a male appearance; This is exacerbated further when, according to genetics, male traits are passed on to female heirs, and vice versa; Under some conditions, the male sex can become attracted to traits formerly not associated with the opposite sex; This can be observed as a sort of sexual Babel effect, in which the popularity of a fat man could promote fat women, a large-chested man could promote large-chested women, etc. With some humor intended, gradually, all women start to appear like dictators of the past; The same does not go for the common man, who is still subject to what are called secondary sex characteristics---that is, characteristics that are not essential to the gene pool; Another such trend is the male identification with the characteristics of the opposite sex; If he is confused or obsessive, he will unconsciously favor desired female traits in his own body; Although this is detrimental to reproduction, it may after all satisfy the man when he is in front of the mirror, just as the obverse condition might do so for a woman; This is what might be called deviously, "conscious evolution," which implies secret rather than overt social and personal development; Obviously, similar traits are bound to be found in the unconscious, where mere prejudices or insults may replace the ostensible operators of functionality, what may be called a 'fascination weakness' or, in a more developed state, a 'mood bias'; It is fascinating to what degree these effects may depend on mere appearance, or aspects of environment, interpreted cognitively::

Prosthetic Recovery - Sometimes a patient can gain some level of recovered function by abandoning some key aspect of reliance or dependence; This is done by adjusting the concept of reality using a prosthetic thesis or "prosthesis"; A baby recovering from a candy addiction could be told "It isn't good for you"; A nymphomaniac could be told "You have better things to do with yourself, something intellectually stimulating" etc.; Prostheses offer the prospect of recovering an earlier, less dangerous concept of reality::

Psyche - In a Cainist system (vis. Oedipus), Psyche would be predated by God, evoking an image of beauty and the beast, radically simplifying and perversifying a field that may otherwise be devoted to sexual fears and history; The depiction of Psyche as a woman suggests not only a man's supposed aggressive urge, but also a degree of weakness and reciprocation which the Christians have called tempta-tion; Thus, in the purest frame of mind it is important to avoid the archetype of the woman Psyche, unless it can be reasoned that a goddess connotes life; Without some sort of belief system in which magic prevails---which may be called irrational---it is difficult to connote life with Psyche, even if some magical exception exists; So, the psychologist's parallel to the mad man's insight on Psyche is that it origi-nates in Ancient Greece::

Psychesis - The action of the psyche; Some feel that this is an intrusive concept, that the soul being relatively perfect, en-gages in no actual action, while others in-cluding Jung and Freud, felt that the psy-che does engage in some active process, or that the activity differs between gender roles; A further position (one that I take), is that the activity of the soul is irrational or hyper-rational, and not all circumstances or positions allow its realization; In this dis-tinction, it is important to differentiate 'mere personality' (however selfish, how-ever defensive) from the true activity of the soul as in many instances a problem solver, or point of animalistic contention; In this sense, the psychologist is confronted with the 'demonism' of not being an ani-mal, or is forced to become an animal also (although some argue that this is relative, categorically it must be absolute; That is, it must be linguistic significance); So the process of psychesis must be distinguished in its high degree of specificity, to individual souls or experiences, and the specific purpose for which it is directed or allocated, be it psychology, say, the faculty of reason, or rather artistic madness or social purpose; Depending on affiliations of judgment, these areas may differ in their degree of consciousness; Only someone with social importance for example, could have social psychesis; But, for those that don't know, social psychesis is possible; This clarifies the main points about psychesis, which is distinguished as a proximate opposite for psychosis; However, various disciplines may ultimately demand that some madness is permissible, say as a demonstration of extreme thought processes; If every form of extremism is evidence of madness, then this leaves psychology with a relatively isolated position on the subject, based on the idea that the soul seeks some kind of dominance; Alternatives to the isolation of psychology sometimes suggest themes influenced by pessimism or naïvete, such as the view that the soul is a drug, or that the brain is a material exception; This opens the way for viewpoints based on social organization, as frequently maintained in biology; The view of the social unconscious seems to provide a double-horned dilemma between telepathic neurosis and biological organization; Biology seems to provide the most convenient excuse for the absence of real telepathic communication, e.g. material subjectivity; Nonetheless, the mind continues to hold authority in areas such as creativity, personality, levels of performance, and politics; If psychology is not a catch-all for evaluations of human behavior, it can be referenced that some specific concepts, such as psychesis, have merit as specific areas of study, yielding knowledge of new domains of reference and association::

Psychic Degeneration - There are several forms of psychic degeneration; Most, I thought, could be treated like arguments which succeed or fail; But it is the special propensity of psychology to house 'monsters' when it comes to pragmatic dilemmas, a notable trend which results in the following list: [1] rhetorical or dialectic failure, [2] personal or emotional failure, [3] monstrous failure / identity failure, [4] circumstantial or associative failure; Indeed, it is even possible to find these attributes in combination.

From a psychologist's point of view it may be difficult to pinpoint exactly which of these is a mental-chemical difficulty and which is purely behavioral, but I think all of these types exist in both kinds, and the list tends to produce less understandable results near the beginning and more behavioral results towards the end;

That is interesting to note, because psychology has often reserved rhetorical standpoints for cursory review, or relegated them to a primitive function; It would be interesting if rhetoric were a primary operator in all of these modes, vis. the formation of identity, the justification of emotion, and the role of association, but I think it is enough to say that rhetoric may be a key variable in certain cases; At least when it is understood that symptoms are a function of treatment;

A secondary form of study is the dynamic role amongst all of these categories, producing experiments like the direct correspondence between rat-like thinking and the presence of labyrinths and the mimicking of historical personalities by relatives of the especially afflicted---a kind of 'art heroism' in place of 'genuine apathy' but the most common case seems to be----as a function of specific objects and life-agendas---that one or two categories at most are fulfilled; This produces artificial differences between the types; Interestingly, sometimes without contingency it is possible to observe that the formation of the soul depends on these kinds of 'human boundaries' for its preservation and reinforcement; Or, alternately, it could be postulated that it is the 'nakedness' of the human spirit which renders it vulnerable to mental disorders and degeneration; The consequent thought, that life should be preserved as some kind of 'illusion', or that function should directly correspond to the relative optimalism of appearances, may seem reproachable, but has a certain degree of merit;

It can be observed that schizophrenic smokers exhibit animal social traits not possessed by schizophrenic non-smokers; If it is an artificial difference it is nonetheless a real category; This shows the proneness to difficulty in the determination of precisely what makes a disease 'apathetic', and precisely what may be determined as a worthwhile recovery; Perhaps life is less honest about matters than the average psychologist believes; In another case, fame for some people means immoral behavior, while to others it means radical functionism; In rare cases, there is overlap; The defining category in some sense represents the development of the soul, and the compatibility with available choices; But if life were dishonest, there would be no direct allegory between a study and the life we personally pursue; So in some sense it is determined that behaviorism relies on the rejection of individuation as a thesis::

Psychic Facts - extends the theory of genuine cause of motivation into a context in which language, facts, and ideas can be motivators (not just agents). Instead of an endless series of agents of effects, there is one consummate effect, not a consummate cause, because it is observed that a cause can have multiple effects; This is a single effect which can have multiple causes; It is called a psychic fact; This is what Jung may have mistaken for the soul---essentially an overwhelming psychological authority, which has little equivalence to a human life; (Nonetheless, the two may interdepend); The importance of psychic facts is not merely organization, it is rather of the form of coherent explanation; People crave to be explained as though the explanation were the sum total of all events or explanations; It is the conventional meaning of coherency, which is actually quite selfish; If there is a genuine explanation, it is that every identity is a set of exceptions, really one identical exception, with an applied correspondence; (Note that in the philosopher's toolkit, correspondence is the opposite of coherency); If all the effects can be explained---if they are not confusing---but the causes cannot be explained completely, then the simple answer is that some---perhaps not all---of the effects are part of some coherent explanation; The interesting point emerges in the case of an endless series of events, in which a coherent or an incoherent explanation is used; Using induction, only an effect is required; Using a posteriori reasoning, similarly a coherent explanation is required; Thus, all that is shared in common between induction and a posteriori is an 'effect of coherent explanation'; Since it has no choice but to work backwards and forwards at the same time---in order to de-tect itself---it can be called a psychic fact; It is merely any effect---not any cause---which has a coherent explanation; Its meaning is open to interpretation, *unless* that interpretation can be explained, in which case we have a theory of motiva-tion::

Psychic Prediction

METHOD 1: Using Opposites

Ask for associations using a specific method; First, ask for the first thing that comes to mind; Then ask 'what is related to this?'; Then ask for 'something differ-ent'; Combine the reverse of the different thing with the related thing from the first question; The result is a factor that is im-portant to the person's life;

[Example 1] The person states that money is meaningful (money is the first thing that comes to mind, and that seems meaning-ful to them); The different thing that comes to mind is 'a secure future'; The conclusion is that 'what may be meaningful to them is the insecurity in their past'; 'Perhaps the key to the financial future lies in dealing with the insecurities of the past';

[Example 2] The person states that love is the first thing that comes to mind, and what they think of is 'curvy women'; What they think of next that is unrelated is driving their motorcycle; The conclusion is something like this: 'You need to think about women who don't ride motorcycles, you need to think about women who aren't riding your motorcycle, and you're secretly afraid they won't like you when you're off your motorcycle; In a way you're afraid that she already owns one; That's the simple answer; If you want a complex answer, then tell me more about your motorcycle'; (Details about the motorcycle are opposite qualities of the woman he would ultimately love, or those opposite qualities represent problems with love he is likely to encounter); See also Superbal Information::

METHOD 2: *Objective Method*

Two categories are opposites, and all other categories are less opposite. One of the two categories is the current condition. The other category is the desired or undesired ultimate conclusion.

Arrange categories like this: A. Initial Condition (two words), then B and C: Two only slightly opposite words from A. which describe a new condition leading to D. and E. F: An opposite condition of A consisting of two words. D and E. a partial opposite condition of the two conditions of F.

Now it can be seen that, if A is to become more opposite (for or against desire), then the result will eventually be D, E, then F. For example, if one is alive, the risk is death or immortality.

If one is a black man, the concern might ultimately be white men or white women.

One is free to disagree with the ultimate context, but the ultimate context is always the opposite. This is the case because the context could be nothing other than the opposite, because no other term expresses the ultimate context of the first condition.

Now let's look at some complete examples.

A. Someone is an effeminate white male, so they think their opposite is a black man. B. and C. To be less white and effeminate, they should study photography with a white woman. This will ultimately lead to conditions which are even less like being effeminate and white. F. The ultimate opposite is perceived as being a black man, in a generic sense. D. and E. For the black man to become a photographer with a white woman, he should have a relationship with an art student. This is also the condition of the effeminate white person who has already studied photography with a white woman, and is becoming more black.

Now it can be predicted, to become black, an effeminate white man should study photography with a white woman and then

215

have a relationship with an art student.

Another example:

A. A black man in prison. Related category
B and C: A white man who wants to be a
police officer, D and E: An actual police
officer, F. A white woman drug addict (the
perceived opposite) somehow involved
with police officers.

Now if the black man wants to get out of
jail, he should have a relationship with a
female drug addict. If the female drug addict wants to go to jail, she should have a
relationship with the man who is already in
jail.

A clearer and much more virtuous method
is to show that when the black man is effeminate in jail, his spiritual experience is
to meet a white lesbian. Similarly, if the
lesbian is feeling effeminate, she is likely
to go to jail, although it may be for religious
reasons.

*METHOD 3: General Method Using Syn-
chronicity*

Every element in life is a predictor; Life is
determined by precedents; For example,
thought is a predictor of original ideas;
Education is a predictor of processes of
advancement; When we look at our everyday lives, what intrigues us is a good pre-

dictor of what events follow immediately after; What is unpredictable is not what types of things happen, but rather their value for us; Predicting value is like predicting how predictable we are, and then copying the values of the past; Value is advanced, however, as it concerns the core meaning of existence;

So, here instead I will give a list of predictors:

Not Going Wilden

But, in a specifically psychic-oriented method, one should be careful 'not to go *wilden*' and crazy. For example, psychic methods may involve knowing when to cover one's ears. But one should not go wilden and assume that one is always psychic. And one should not go wilden and always cover one's ears. That about sums up the wilden concept.

METHOD 4: Practical Method

A relation between events and words and circumspection. Words determine events. If one hears particular words which sound (to you) like they are from the deep south of the United States, then you are more likely to have some relationship with the deep south of the United States. Your current position determines what type of relationship this is. For example, if you live in

France, you may visit the southern United States. If you are just being born, then you may find your parents are from the southern United States. But the more discerning you are, the more likely the words are less significant, and you are able to correct the situation. For example, you may determine that your parents are from the deep south of the United States, but you yourself live in New Haven, CT where you were born after they moved to New Haven for your dad's dissertation work. Intelligence, or some amount of story-making, becomes the missing link between absurd explanations, and what actually happens.

PSYCHIC PREDICTION CHART

GENERALLY: Extreme translates as typical, and vice versa, except in dreams. Emotional prediction is basically color prediction.

REAL LIFE : FUTURE PREDICTION
Thinking about Hitler: See blond men;
Thinking about money: See armored cars;
Thinking about movies: See news headlines;
Dream about history: Get noticed;
See structure: Create structure;
See emotions: Encounter drama;
Feel emotional: Life changes;
Feel haughty: Encounter challenges;
Feel aroused: Time remains;
Take medicine: Have control or space;
Break leg: Regain something temporarily;
Find a coin: Valued participation;

SENSITIVITY: The children of sensitive parents love furniture. Parents, however, are more likly than other people to stuff strange furniture into the car. The parents are predicting disaster, the kids are predicting love. Objectivity + Sensitivity = Development.

The psychic difference is merely if the factors are noticed, not whether they occur. If signs don't seem to appear, it means that the central obsession of the personality has not consciously manifested, or perhaps the individual is in poor health::

Psychic Preferences - are differentiated at least into male and female types; By this I mean specific feelings which may be considered as the exclusive indicators of psychic---that is---purely mental patterns of thought, differentiated from language, and differentiated from the classifications of phenomena which are functions of language; In the male it can be observed for example, especially in the following phenomena:

> Reaction-Time
> Inexorable, Inevitable
> Streamlining
> Perfectability, Technicalism

In the female, an entirely different, but potentially related set of emotions forms:

> Empathy
> Euphenia
> Synchronicity
> Serendipity

It is worth noting that when one type resembles another, or when there is sexual intercourse, the two types may merge or share characteristics; However, this is partly explained by communication between the types;

The types of psychic preferences, whatever they happen to be, may be further divided into general and specific types; The general types relate to viable coherent states of mind, while the specific types may reflect some specialized understanding, such as a correspondence to a specific type of entity (or idea); Correspondence between general and specific function may then strengthen a particular modus of development in psychic function::

Psychic Psychology - is not widely talked about; But the prevalence of sophisticated drugs and the emergence of biotechnology promises to change this; The interface between the functioning brain and computer augmentations will serve to enhance thought; The very nature of the landscape is changing to accommodate the experiences of those privileged enough to interface with computers; One need only look to the very recent emergence of internet cafes; In my book, *The Dimensional Philosopher's Toolkit*, I describe a system that can be used as an objective interface and reasoning tool; These sorts of tools will only be improved by the concurrence of chemical treatments; In the future, the most competent forms of reasoning will intersect on consumer technology, creating different layers of parallel between functional / dysfunctional consumer and functional / dysfunctional technology; At this juncture it is important to realize that at the minimum we must preserve the func-

tionality of one or the other; Perhaps there
will be one day when technology is not
seen as the 'soulless machines' that some
post-apocalyptic thinkers have thought
them to be.

PSYCHIC TECHNIQUES:

Predicting the Present · gains in perspective and
  forecasting that can occur at many levels,
  increases exponentially with living in the future;
Determining Opportunity - Knowing the artificiality
  of existence;
Living the Future - allows one to enact future goals
  and ideas;
Luck - may improve with conventional partly self-
  determined factors; Increases exponentially with
  psychic significance;
Psychic Focus - combining predicting the present and
  living the future, this opens the possibility of true
  psychic perceptions, which may be unconscious
  without luck or strong determination;
Psychic Significance - beginning with arbitrary rules,
  key objects and ruminations can be associated
  with the individual, creating meaningful
  correspondences; Improves with psychic spirit;
Psychic World - building on psychic focus, there is
  sometimes dangerous connection to the true
  underpinnings of reality, which can be mastered
  with formalities, but is usually subtle and depends
  on significance;
Psychic Spirit - psychic identity or spirit begins to
  emerge when there is opportunity to focus on
  psychic significance; This may depend on
  involvement in psychic decisions or perceptions;
  Varying levels exist corresponding to necessary
  versus determinate forms of influence;

Further Levels - may include magic, future
  prediction, or magical character, but often these
  levels, like the previous, are subject to a large
  but not absolute number of exceptions::

Psychic Techniques -

::

Psychic Techniques and Ersatz Vectors
- Someone shows anger after not being
given a stimulant. However, the anger in
this case is not expressed to be a response to jealousy. But if others would assume it could reasonably be jealousy,
could we not also say that the anger was a
psychic response to not receiving the
stimulant? Traditionally there is 'no way' of
mapping so-called 'subtle' responses to
stimulation or lack thereof; But, under ersatz vectors, clearly there is a reasonable
case for scheming out a causal relation,
and adducing some set of patterned responses, even over a large area of data;

Consider, for example, that social scien-
tists have conditioned responses to social
data, and mobile citizens may have a
'nominal-topical' response to a stimulation
concept, whether or not they receive it;
Then there is a case (when there is a direct correlation between data and identity),
for a correspondence between data-
identity and identity itself; Clearly these
interactions between data and identity are
a response to some kind of meme concept, or perhaps something more simple;

While not psychic in a spiritual sense, the
use of ersatz vectors may prove psychic in
an informational sense; Thus, the
prospend (intended position) that psychic
data is spiritual may be recognized as an

224

unchecked assumption that has little directly to do with psychic legitimacy; Much as a magician must over-think his audience, within certain conditions complex evidence does not fly in the face of provability; Usually by using one-point connections, a direct causal link can be determined, either by property (say, in logic, a property that is fully correlated), by establishing a certain probability (this is a basis for probability theory), or finally by establishing a necessary logical correspondence, using logical conditioning;

Links such as those between taken-for-granted data and causal relations, between full probabilities and category relations, or between systemic relation and applied logic are examples of ersatz vectors which have a near- psychic influence on some patterns in information, through an initial one-degree certainty supporting two degrees of partial affirmation; The fashionably weak thesis of this possible system is that it only refers to information, not opinion; But as such it is well-suited to the objective psychologist;

Such a theory (ersatz vectoring) should not depend on falsifiable theories; Thus, it may be useful to condition properties using a relativistic (suppositional) or qualifiable framework; It may be considered that the potential for qualities is not falsifiable in the abstract, because some reasoning could be acquired for them; This follows from a complexivist view that all potentialities are real in the sense of having influence upon knowledge; If there are quantity variables, they should refer to an exclusive context which is considered to be a premise of any conclusions that follow; If the context is not exclusive, it becomes difficult to determine the objective (true) nature of what is being said;

A *Second Technique of Ersatz Vectors* incorporates a double contingency, so that for example in the case of 'taking a shower because one uses a drug', if this is affirmed, then the negation is disconfirmative, so the result of negation would be to affirm the statement that 'not taking a shower is not a result of using a drug'; Although not coherent or absolute, combining multiple of these types of statements could provide evidence against incoherency::

Psychological Agency Dilemmas -

Problem of John	Problem of Aphid
Problem of Jack	Problem of Vivian

I have used names to express archetypes of agency problems which occur to nearly everyone; ("Agency" means problems of will or personality, often divided into the categories of human intelligence and artificial intelligence);

Problem of Aphid: To do something, to make some impression;

Problem of John: To accomplish something, to make some progress;

Problem of Jack: To do everything, to be satisfied;

Problem of Vivian: To be vivacious, to be successful;

Psychological Deduction - Unlike the philosophical version of this technique, it is variablist---the mote in the center is replaced with a reference variable, and the process is consequently linear-constructive, moving from a defined panel, to an opposite-defined panel, to a context panel, to the remaining context panel---what a philosopher would call 'asymmetric';

A central point of definition is defined, usually "desire", but sometimes "emotion" or "development". Usually the upper half of the diagram refers to the 'client's perspective' and the lower half refers to the 'therapist's perspective'. The context panels, defined by the upper right and lower left, are developments of the initial opposite perspective.

Here is a context in which the client has defined that what is 'desired' is "transformation":

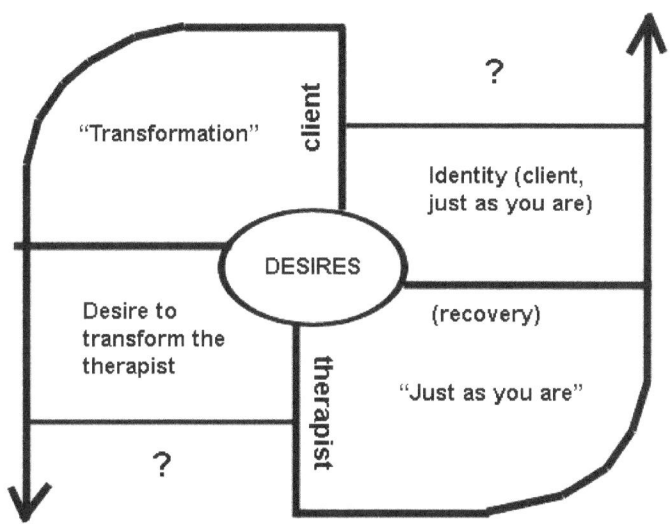

[A copy-able template can be found in the final Appendix (Templates)]

It can be assumed, in the first place, that the client projects the conflict upon the therapist, so the therapist is always presented as having an opposite position (this can be used as a general rule in these diagrams). However, this opposite position is important in defining how the client may develop.

In this case, the client's desire for transformation is projected into the desire to transform the therapist, which presents the initial conflict in the lower left panel. The

229

therapist's desire for the client to recover 'just as he or she is' becomes the priority for the client to transform in terms of his or her own already-existing identity.

Now we can look at the remaining panels, where the question marks have been written. How does the client develop the desire to transform the therapist?

Client: "I want the therapist to realize that he doesn't have an opinion"
Response (opposite): "This means you should develop your opinions about other things"

How does the therapist develop the desire to transform the patient 'just as he or she is'?

Therapist: "I want the client to self-actualize"
Response (opposite): "The therapist should 'actualize' therapy"

Another example: The client's desire is to recover past memories, and when pressed about their feeling on this, the client responds that they feel resistant:

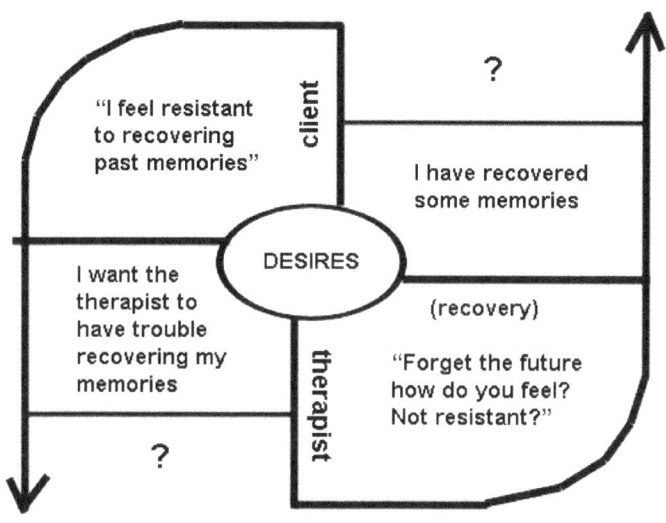

[A copy-able template can be found in the final Appendix (Templates)]

Here the therapist's generally opposite statement to repressed memories is precisely the statement that allows memories to be recovered: "Forget the future, how do you feel? Not resistant?".

The client's resistance to recovering memories expresses as the desire for the therapist to have trouble recovering the memories, which is a kind of confusion about responsibility. The therapist's opposite statement directly (or gradually) results in the recovery of the patient's traumatic experiences, assuming he or she had any.

Now we look at the question mark panels. What does the client think about the therapy?:

Client: "The therapist can't recover the memories for me"
Response (opposite): "It is possible for you to recover the memories"

What does the therapist have to say about the patient, translating the recovery of memories?

Therapist: "I understand the patient's position. It's a smooth road with bumps"
Response (opposite): "I don't understand my memories. It's all bumpy and I want it smoothed out"

At this point, the therapist can recommend therapy, which is par for the course;

The deductive method can also be used, as mentioned earlier, with development and emotional concerns, in which, if emotional, it may be important to address opinions about the therapist, and if developmental, to consider what it would be like if just the opposite of events had happened. Since the only case in which the individual has a completely negative opposite is one in which the patient is paradigmatic, there is little risk of concerning oneself with negative issues instead of positive ones. If the patient has positive developments, he or she may want to feel more confident by appreciating what went missing when the positives appeared.

Relationships such as 'constructive / deconstructive' and happiness / sadness can be understood in terms of the desire of the therapist to understand the patient, and bring about recovery. For example, if the therapist cannot deconstruct the patient's happiness, he or she is forced to deconstruct the patient's sadness; This desire on the part of the therapist should bring happy feelings in the patient, so long as it is understood that the therapist accepts the patient's emotions. Insisting on deconstructing sadness is actually a very effective approach to happy patients, just as feeling happy for someone may be an effective response to sadness, when it is a genuine emotion. The response in this case with some interpretation is that the patient wants the therapist to feel happy, and the therapist needs to feel the pathos. The barrier may simply be that the patient doesn't understand that the therapist is capable of happiness (that 'happiness is possible'). If the therapist feels happy for the sad patient, the therapist can address whether the patient feels unemotional, or if there is some way in which the therapy has been insensitive. If the therapy is not the concern, the central issue can be changed to something like 'responsibility' or 'transformation'. In this way, the process can become constructive even when there are barriers. Emotions should not be the concern if they can only be viewed in a negative light, independent of who is having them; That points towards a structural concern rather than a concern of understanding::

Psychological Fallacy - The study of psychology has many benefits for therapy. However, if we were to be critical, what precisely could be wrong with psychology? One argument is that psychology is only as wrong as the human mind is flawed. However, this ignores the specifics of applying psychology. Perhaps *if there is a problem* it relates with the ineffability or immaterialism of psychology. If a psychologist admits that he is an immaterialist, what does this say about the nature of therapy? It may seem like 'no wonder' that patients' dreams do not materialize, or that many find individual or group therapy unsatisfying or 'empty'. So, that, apparently, is the only major problem with psychology, other than a material one, which is that psychology has been obsessed with the ineffable. If there were another problem it might be the traditional assumption that psychology obsesses over problems, and over-diagnoses patients. It can be seen that if that were the case, there would be more instances of 'miracle cures' than are reported today.

Psychological Knowledge and the Tractatus of Psychology

Basic Knowledge Using Categories:
(A) Environment, noun; (B) Macro adjective; (C) Problem adjective; (D) Environmental curiosity, noun;

Then combine into (1) A : B :: C : D,
(2) A : D :: B : C;

The result gives something that should be basic knowledge in the context of the person's life;

Psychic Knowledge Using Categories:
(A) Emotional subject, (B) Most common fault with that subject, (C) What is impossible about this subject?, (D) What is the quality of this impossibility?;

Then combine into (1) B:C :: A:D, (2) B:A :: D:C

Continuing with the psychic knowledge method, the general problems in therapy can be ranked according to which are most serious, from most to least serious:

235

THE TRACTATUS OF PSYCHOLOGY:

1. You don't want reality to be the problem;
2. You don't want the emotion to be identical with the impossibility (category 3); You want the emotion to be something appealing, but if it's too evil, you're back to the reality problem; Then you might as well assume that the fault (category 2) is a denial of something in category 1, unless you have something good to feel good about;
3. Impossibility (category 3) also shouldn't be an extension of category 1 (emotion); There should be a sense of insight about impossibility in every person, even if this thing is something humorous; Irrationality about the impossible in the form of highly specific 'impossibilities' may be healthy for personality;
4. Also, the quality of impossibility (category 4) should not be the opposite or extension of the fault of emotion (category 2), as this will produce conflicts of personality;

SOLUTION TYPES RELATING TO THE
TRACTATUS OF PSYCHOLOGY:

SOLUTION CASE 1: SIMPLE TRUTH
(A) Me, (B) Where I live, (C) Nothing, (D) I
don't know; Translation: I live nowhere and
I don't know myself, or I live in me and
there is nothing I don't know; How to address this person: Is it possible that you're
taking too many risks in this life you live? If
not, it's possible you don't need therapy.

SOLUTION CASE 2: COMMUNICATING
TRUTH: (A) Insincerity, (B) Self, (C) Ego,
(D) Emotion; Translation: Your ego has an
insincere emotion, or you are insincere
with your emotions or ego. How to address
this person: You seem to have the right
priorities; In the future we'll take a look at
your life from your perspective, assuming
you want to continue.

SOLUTION CASE 3: INTELLIGENT
TRUTH: (A) Irony, (B) Bitterness, (C)
Epiphany, (D) Truth; Translation: The bitter
epiphany is that irony is truth, or the bitter
irony is that truth is an epiphany; How to
address this person: You're certainly intelligent but it's possible there are some
things you don't know about yourself. Do
you dream?

SOLUTION CASE 4: AMBITIOUS TRUTH:
(A) Danger, (B) Intuition, (C) Philosophy,
(D) Myself; Translation: Intuitive philosophy is dangerous to yourself, or there is a
dangerous intuition in your own philosophy; How to address this person: You certainly have motivations. We'll look into
what you want and the sense of your life;
We will address any problems of guilt or
inferiority that you may have.

*PROBLEM TYPES RELATING TO THE
TRACTATUS OF PSYCHOLOGY:*

PROBLEM CASE 1 (characterized by consisting of a theory of a problem): INFOR-
MATION PROBLEM: Example: (A) Science, (B) Statistical, (C) Gray areas, (D)
Subjectivity; Translation: The statistics of
gray areas is the science of subjectivity, or
the statistical science is the gray area of
subjectivity; How to address this person: It
seems like you have some serious thinking
to do.

PROBLEM CASE 2 (characterized by ambiguous definitions): UNSOLVED
THOUGHTS: Example: (A) Reality, (B)
Emotion, (C) Nothing or everything, (D)
Confusion; Translation: Emotion is nothing
or everything to you, and reality is confusing, or the emotional reality is that nothing
or everything is confusing; How to address
this person: Decide what is important to
you, and you will have a new sense of
clarity.

PROBLEM CASE 3 (characterized by a
paradox): SELF-INSTATED CONFUSION:
(A) Sanity, (B) Madness, (C) Madness, (D)
Clarity; Translation: The madness of madness is the clarity of sanity, or the madness of sanity is the clarity of madness;
How to address this person: Sanity is
really different from madness unless your
brain is completely different from every-
body else.

PROBLEM CASE 4 (characterized by an
identification with difficult, problematic subjects B and D): EMOTIONAL DIFFI-
CULTY : (A) Insensitivity, (B) Cruelty, (C)
Love, (D) Loneliness; Translation: Cruel
love is insensitive to loneliness, or cruel
insensitivity loves loneliness; How to address this person: Think of something
more positive by re-defining your emotional subject.
::

239

Psychological Location - Initially in parsing out the notion of psychological (mental)
location, I thought of four concepts: location of fixation, monstrous location, non-
location, and equinymous location; Although these serve the important role of
mapping specific areas of weakness in
psychology, the choices are less accomplished in structured or constructive areas;
A more conventional approach, which I
later followed, is dealt in terms of entity
iconization; These alternate categories
roughly sketch-out the established and un-
established areas of location, from individual identity:

independ-ent	construct-ive
logical or emotional	transc-endent or creative

The first (constructive) is social, trial-and-
error, and authority-based; The second
(independent) is free-willed and individual,
and explorative; The third (logical or emotional) is the space projected to and from
others; The fourth type (transcendent or
creative) is about accessory realities and
growth or stagnation of other forms of location; See also Positer Characteristics::

240

Psychology (New) -

Symbolic locations have activity techniques; Symbolic activities have located techniques::

Psychology Prima - is in one sense the tools and methods employed by the therapist, such as suppression and (recovery) techniques; However, in another sense the primary or prima aspects of psychology relate only to functional psychology; This might be derided as idealistic or naïve, until it is discovered that some people do have problems which are not only dysfunctional, but are unpleasant and undesirable; However, some say, if any condition were universally undesirable, the Nazis would have won; There is a debate as to whether the conditions of life are ever agreed to, or whether there is what is called 'widespread coping'; If the coping is not agreeable, this throws a cruel animalistic light on sexuality, otherwise it is possible sometimes to maintain that life is contractual; So, psychology prima might be answered with 'what is a valid contract?', 'how is life contracted?' or else 'what is the manner or behavior of coping?'; Another approach is to dismiss difficulty in general, calling it an artificial subject, as some might do from a position of privilege; But some of these people might still be open to 'talk strategy', bringing the argument full circle; However, if psychology is not strategic, it become alienated from the popular notion of self-control or social influence; This is seen more fully when the absence of strategy is defined chemically, for it is possible that a strategic concept of psychology is objectual and not ever completely chemical, whereas chemical psychology is the type most likely to lack control; For example, if a perfect mind had chemistry, it might be attributed to reality rather than thoughts, otherwise it is clear that there must be no relation between thought and reality, hence it could become irrational; For this and other reasons, schizophrenia becomes intellectually appealing to the psychologist, unless a semantic argument is adopted to blur the boundary between the chemical and the real; However, clearly there are people---e.g. brain-damaged people or highly exceptional people---who have one and not the other; Thus it is really impossible to adopt the semantic argument without some dishonesty which then enters the practice of therapy::

Psychosomatics - Psychosomatic pain is most typically triggered by the suppression of the numbing of pain; The psychosomatic pain increases with the number of times the pain is remembered, as the brain has difficulty reasoning, first that the pain occurred, but was numbed, and second that the pain did not occur a second time without a second numbing; Other cases called spectral pain (commonly 'spectral limbs') are responses to extreme pain that was not originally numbed; The brain fails to recognize where the pain occurred, because the degree of pain experienced confused the sensation in the first place; The un-locatedness of the pain is exacerbated by a poor memory, while the vividness of the experienced is exacerbated by the degree of pain felt originally; The role of imagination in the processes is secondary to the cause, but may play a role of enhancing the apparent significance of the trauma; Overcoming the event in serious cases may involve re-attachment to the pleasures of life that happened before the pain occurred, or else an intelligent form of denial, combined with the confrontation of physical rather than psychological fear; The condition should be distinguished from phobias; In the case of phobias, the cause is attachment to the symptoms or else some underlying difficulty, rather than a problem with physical pain and memory::

Psychosophy - is distinguished from psychology, if at all, by its pursuit of comprehensive knowledge not only of the patient, but of the meaningful egress upon therapy, embracing the entire experience as though it could be a worthwhile end-in-itself; Psychosophy is distinguished from philosophy in its adoption of feelings or psychic indicators to express what may be knowledge of people, pathologies, or social psychology;

243

Psychosophy asks the therapist to experience, thrive, and even indulge in experiences which may be unpleasant in their origin and manifestation; This involves a certain degree of tacit knowledge which must be honed from a seemingly endless series of rather or almost personal encounters with others' minds and attitudes; One should be careful that these experiences are adequate for knowledge, a claim a philosopher cannot always make, and simultaneously that the series of encounters is not a rollercoaster ride that merely indulges personal beliefs; Indeed, the psychosoph must rely on clinical accounts, through which she or he must intertwine his or her own threads of psychological theory; It is the joinery of personal and objective assessments which promises to open and reveal a larger world, the world of real knowledge of the psyche::

================R===============

Rank, Otto - One of the most modern of the early psychologists, he wrote on themes such as sex and the unconscious; He is famous for his book, *The Doppleganger*, explaining the concept of 'the double', a way of moderating Freud's theories of the ego, the Id, and the Super-Ego; Later in life he issued a detraction of Freud, in which he said: "Such a detached attitude may be justified in the realm of pure science, that is, of theoretical psychology, but is certainly contrary to all therapeutic endeavors, which ought to aim towards life itself"::

Rational Semantics -

Less rational-functional people tend to go through the following cycle:

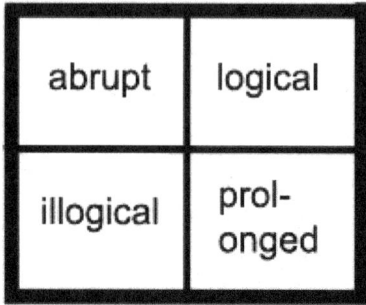

abrupt	logical
illogical	prol-onged

They are stuck at this level due to their level of thinking (never mention this to the patient).

When this thinking changes, then they sometimes succeed in attaining a higher level, such as the level of the Unitarian. And sometimes they simply fail to achieve this one. The danger of perversity and anger, and addiction for example, is to compromise the advantages which accommodate this level. It is then no accident that these sorts of behaviors often occur in order to secure some advantage.

At this level, people tend to believe that the only form of reason is logic, and the result follows a four-stage process (as indicated by the diagram): (1) Seeking logic-as-reason, there is a dependence on logic rejecting logic (i.e. through incoherency, etc.) leads to the second stage; (2) The person tries singing, blurting, criticism, etc. When the result is questioned, he or she begins to see themselves as irrational. (3) Testing the system, the individual tries some irrational things to gain information. When this information is inconclusive, the person is left with: (4) Prolonged activities, including obsessions and boredom::

Realization - On a holistic level, this may take place in a paroxysm [see Index under Paroxysm]; Pragmatically, however, there are other methods or 'incidents' which may be either linguistic or sensual; These form complexes which may be participated in, in a manner that may be arbitrated in partial or complete form;

The Aphoristic Complex seeks linguistic results, thus it is initially 'wise'; At times this may seem to capture all complexes of realization;

The Associative Complex seeks sensual satisfaction in proportion to memory, but may be degenerative; It has a reputation for 'age' or 'life';

The Sophisticated Complex is often

247

comparative; Some view it wrong-fully as a degenerate impulse; Al-though it may be endemic to ques-tions of dysfunction, its results are constructive for realization::

Reassurance -

Reassurance As a Self-Sustaining Cycle

It is not absolutely bad	It doesn't end immediately
The effect is not permanent	It is not gone forever

Diagram reads C.C. from upper right;

According to the diagram, the opposite of reassurance is shock, incrimination, time, and death.

Positive factors for reassurance are flu-ency, success, connection, and vitality.

Compare with the types of Regret::

Recovery Techniques - or Freudian re-emergence has been criticized as brutal and labor-intensive, resulting in any case in two conditions, which may be adjusted according to the standard of sensitivity: (1) The condition in question is said to be serious, and (2) The manner of analysis is to touch on it gently, without bringing it to consciousness for more than a 'lightning instant'; Clients are then advised to re-visit their discoveries of trauma, primitive beliefs, or sexual knowledge on their own time, when they feel most comfortable to re-visit the material; In Freud's tradition, the most valuable method for reaching recovery (say of specific images or thought-experiences) was to ask probing questions and then assess through an examination of accidental words, what the patient really, and deeply, meant; While this process is gradual, it is ultimately rewarding and a highly accurate portrayal of the subject's mental experiences; According to a dimensional theory, questioning may follow a course that is subject to rules of inference, for example, especially opposite potential qualities observed in the client; It may follow from agreeable/unpredictable to sensitive/insensitive to passive/violent; The progression from one stage to the next gives clues about the client's basic motivations and specific life intentions; Recovery occurs when the client himself becomes aware of the hidden dialectic; If the client becomes obfuscatory, it may be

249

stated plainly to them that they are being insincere or dishonest; A technique may be also used of asking the client to imagine or "think about" what he or she is saying; Further insight may be had by referring to experiences the client has talked about, if necessary; Some of the information should already be discussed, during an initial interview, or by reminding the client about what has been discussed before; See also Suppression Technique::

Regret (Types of)-

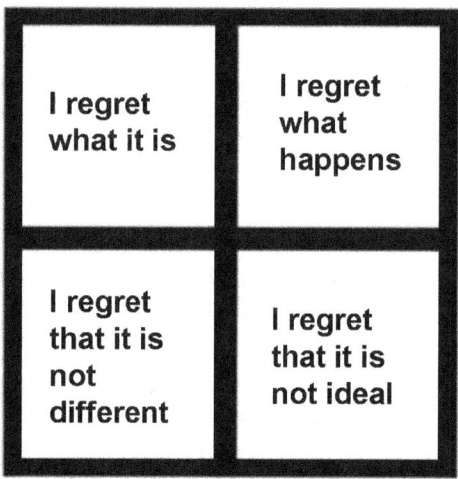

| I regret what it is | I regret what happens |
| I regret that it is not different | I regret that it is not ideal |

The above stages are of increasing maturity, if it is realized that there are four corresponding ways to change thinking:

A. The first stage (corresponding to the upper right box), even if it is a disaster, is not a total disaster, at least usually;
B. The second stage (referring to the upper left corner) is unproductive;
C. The third stage (corresponding to the lower left box) authenticates the person;
D. The fourth stage (the lower right box) is only necessary when it is constructive;

With that, the patient is better able to handle regret; However, he or she may not necessarily always be mentally prepared to shift thinking; In that case, it would be better to address each category individually, discussing the concerns in an accepting way, and making gentle note of the limitations of the current perspective

Compare with types of Reassurance::

The **Religion of Adequacy** is a prevalent thought for professors and students; Only the doctor receives special reassurance of total purposefulness; In this sense it is the religion of doctors; But what is its functional psychology for those without an M.D.?; Evidently individuals are forced to pyramid their lives on a basis of health and recoverability; If it were mandated that health were the only structure of life, we are left with a paradigm of measuring up to 'super-powers' that for whatever reason fulfill the necessary criteria to dominate the variables; What happens if these individu-

als, for whatever reason, are dysfunctional? (Say, by our own private personal
standard?); Then we turn to less obviously
functional 'exceptional' personalities for a
sense of adequacy; In some ways the
paradigms for 'love', 'cuteness', and some
forms of fetishes cater to this opinion that
exception is the guide of life; But, ultimately, if no exception or super-power ful-
fills the promise of health, we are left with
a religion of adequacy in which the adequate is all that anyone can achieve::

Research Psychology - I take a futurist
approach to the research of psychology;
Not only is psychology adapted to the aesthetic of its times---a theory that can be
said to affect sexuality and life choices
amongst other things---but the formal aspects of mental imagery, indeed the stuff
of psychology itself, is continually being
refined; By this I don't mean a cup full of
sugar; I mean that psychological research
depends not only on case studies, which
have the quality of timelessness, but also
futuristic methods suited to the exact moment in history; (If anything, theories
should be more futuristic, not less, except
when considering the faults of history);
Even if some of these methods question
the soundness of previous cases, the general growth is one for broader perspectives
and better judgment; In this endeavor the
principle of conservation is simply the validity of a present thesis; It is what might

be called open psychology, working with the basic principle that it is inadequate to inspire fear---fear is dysfunctional; See Future Psychology::

Rhetorical Psychology (Dimensional Experimentation) -

Thesis: *Both sanity and madness can be meaningful;*

Inquiry: *But what decides this?*

Stipula: *It is undecided if either are trivial, because meaning could be trivial;*

Resulting Diagram:

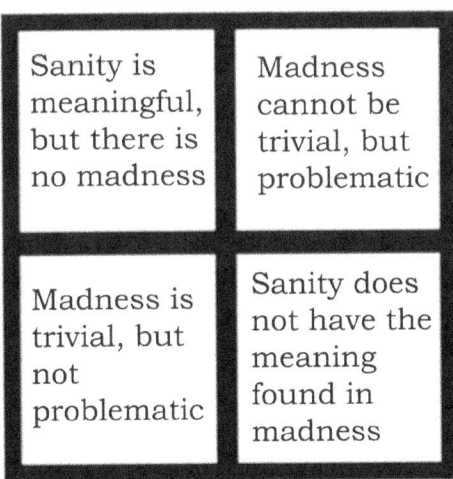

Sanity is meaningful, but there is no madness	Madness cannot be trivial, but problematic
Madness is trivial, but not problematic	Sanity does not have the meaning found in madness

(Read counter-clockwise from upper-right)

The evident result is something like a decision on the triviality of madness, or the exclusion of one or the other concept; (I consider this constructive); The result can then be used to develop survey questions where the control is variable(s) such as language ability, age, or creative impulse, resulting in a measure of universability;

FYI: The variables 'sanity' and 'madness' can be meaningfully replaced with potentially reasonable or potentially unreasonable claims, resulting in a more complex comparison, and a means to cross-reference qualities and aspects which are not at first considered to be related; If this results in neutral areas, I would advise keeping an eye towards the inherent functionality of the neutrals; E.g. 'isn't citizenship a neutral concept', 'not to everyone' then the cycle repeats and more data is fed into the system, by parsing sane and mad variations of citizenship (or some other supposed neutral concept)::

Rift in Reality - A major question is raised in psychology as to how accurately experiences represent a common reality, even in an outward sense; It is clear that if reality were the same, it would be identical; But as such, does that mean that two people would share the same body?; Would they compete for importance?; There are examples in language which raise the issue directly, such as, does the tactical game

Counter-Strike mean a worker's strike to the older generation?; One response is to ridicule the question; But then again, the older generation *does* have different experiences, doesn't it?; If it does, then why not find a common significance for the signifier?; If it doesn't have different experiences, then it is as though they are the same people; This can be solved by memes in some cases, such as that the declaration (to play) Counter-Strike as 'enmattered' in the idea that it was a counter-top game; However, this entails a certain degree of simple-faction; In such a position, every reference structure is considered independently coherent, so that there is no subjective case without specifically applied information; The only uncle that thinks there's a strike is the one looking over your shoulder while you play the game, or use whatever other reference is appropriate to your case; (This is a response to what is called the fallacy of reference or the fallacy of deference); Clearly most of the differences which may be raised in a rift of reality, whether they are generational, technical, or personal, may be called 'topical' differences, which as such depend on the specifics of reference structure; Thus there is a thesis in which differences of reality are also differences in understanding; For otherwise the difference between realities becomes undiscernible, and the result is a meaningless case::

Rituals - are a frequent motif of psychological experiences; Four common types emerge, often in relation to music, which has been an early communicator of tribal authority and hence belief:

(1) Ritual accompanied by music; Such is the familiar 'doo doo doo doo' heard on cultural anthropology programs, (2) Spiritual ritual, often mimicking a travel towards death or paradise; This often has incorporated a concept of superstitious 'noiseless sound' as made popular by Hollywood and far-eastern movies, and documentaries which depict mandalas interspersed with images of the Buddha, etc., (3) Genuinely noiseless experiences have a kind of non-existent or self-constructed music, (4) Subtle noises such as chimes or pouring water often act as signs of initiation, and may be seen as an architectural or cultural motif;

Certainly, it can be seen that the four aspects offer a kind of coherent picture of ritual-nature: (A: 1-3) Travel, described as a presence or absence of sound, which may be a strategic spiritual quest, and (B: 2-4) Knowledge or ecstasy, described as ambiguous or tender noises; These can be likened to the difference between ordinary conversation and intimate love::

Ritual Functions - may be one of the simplest methods of understanding a patient, the moments at which the patient's actions are most transparent; Simple associations overlap like a macramé, producing instances in which simple motivations are expressed unconsciously; And ritual function is by no means a restrictive designation; It applies largely to all forms of dialogue and willful and unwillful communication; Any personal representation which may be symbolic may be a form of ritual; One may also look to "clear moments" the patient has, and when the moment seems clear to the patient, unconscious feelings are also clearly expressed; This is very similar to the unconscious revelation of words explained by Freud::

Rogers, Carl - the progenitor of a passive approach to therapy, in which patients gradually realize their own inner desires and motivations, and learn to act upon them in ways that are reinforced by positive relationships in which there is consciousness of the psychological drive::

The Rot of the Soul, and the Solutions -

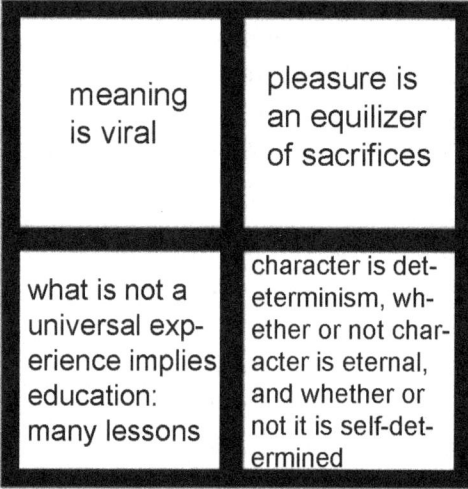

meaning is viral	pleasure is an equilizer of sacrifices
what is not a universal experience implies education: many lessons	character is determinism, whether or not character is eternal, and whether or not it is self-determined

::

Rote Disorders - A broader theme than obsession or compulsion, re-iterating the theme of a modifiable variable; These are problems that are neither genetic nor chemical; Instead, they may be described as "habits"; While this may mean that the disorder is less serious, some fraction of the symptoms of a chemical or genetic disorder may sometimes be ascribed to rote: that is, norms and equalities which circumvent the individual's genuine and innate desires.

===============S================

Sacrificial Dilemma - Medical practitioners are often faced with difficult choices between a patient's long term and short-term health, the risk involved in surgery, the side-effects of medication, etc.; These may exist at the design level as well as, to some extent, on the clinical treatment level; But these choices have roots in sacrifices intrinsic to the patients' lives---be they genetic, principled, or hedonistic commitments, or a simple unscrupulousness with accidents; In a dimensional system it is important to treat sacrifices as originating within a context of real commitments, and therefore to act (subtly, in proportion to resourcefulness) against unnecessary forms of life commitment; This has the potential to inform preventative measures which may be important in psychology; Some people, for example, may commit without a principle, becoming uncontrollable liars, bullies, or hypochondriacs simply because it serves a whim; While the alternative may look like paranoia---perhaps it is only some form of chemical stimulus which informs these behaviors---sometimes false commitments have a chaotic effect upon others' lives, when it is assumed that every life choice begins with commitment; So, either one must commit to principled origins of ill-effect, such as

259

the idea that liars are concealing some aspect of their lives, or one must commit to a chaotic origin of some commitments within pathology; These two options suggest two routes for dimensionism: [1] A "top-down" dimensionism beginning with functional categories (see the Allegorical) or [2] A "bottom-up" dimensionism beginning with the highly specific nature of individuals; This points towards abbreviating pathology into "modes" and "perspectives" lending inevitably to some functional overlap (See also Mode Pathology and Perspective Pathology), and the critical distinction that perspectives should have an adequate mode and vice versa::

Safeguards and Tactics - There are a number of general techniques which prove beneficial in the context of rehabilitating the patient to their natural environment, that is, to the most functional platform of thought; Although combining two or three of these might be self-contradictory, one or two might add punch or spice to what may be futilistic attitudes in therapy; Not only do these allow the therapist to modulate the experience, but they promote the patient's ability for self-control or self-modulation:

(1) *Encouragement*: As a general rule, the default character of interaction is one of encouragment; Specific encouragements should be guided to appeal to the specific interests and motivations of the patient,

whenever these activities are healthy for the patient's development; Attention can be paid to passivity versus excitement;

(2) *Reverse Psychology*: Patients or clients who deal with dishonest feelings or simply need to work out problems for themselves may benefit by a mild inquiring tone, unexpected compliments, or exaggerated interest in some subjects; This may be especially useful in confidence-building, or to reassure the patient that the therapist 'is real'; When the patient questions reality this may often be a reflection of early experiences with dishonesty, which need to be addressed; As an alternative to reverse psychology, theories can be used to create new prospective territories of discussion;

(3) *Sage Advice*: Obvious advice should be saved for obvious and dangerous topics, whereas subtle advice should be given freely on the occasion of the importance of subtle or unconscious topics; In general, advice is not the role of the therapist, but ironically it may be necessary, and has at least subtle and obvious dimensions of importance;

(4) *Specification*: Consider that when golden eagle means gold (or motorcycles) the patient is not afraid of golden eagles; Thus, when the patient encounters fear of golden eagles when golden eagles have been attributes to gold or motorcycles,

261

there is a higher chance of an actual fear of motorcycles or gold, rather than eagles; In some cases (of mild anxiety) promoting this awareness of labels can eliminate fear of the primary object; Reverse psychology can be used to supplement for cases where specification backfires::

Sanity -

Levels of Sanity:

Sanguine Temper-ament	Sober
Devotee	Divine Empir-icism

Sanity in Language:

Parsim-ony	Speaking in Tong-ues
Speaking Mind	Eloq-uence

::

Methods of Sanity

Intelligent Activities, especially talking, memory, and public speaking, as well as reading, writing, and drawing.

Practicing Silence through stillness-of-mind exercises.

Personal Growth through Incremental Steps. This can help to recover lost abilities.

Also, it may help to practice calmness and avoid urgency about the more important things in life. The longer one is willing to wait, so goes the rule, the sooner good things are likely to arrive.

Seasonology - Someone may beat their chest and say 'boomba boomba'; And someone will reply half-jokingly 'Well, then that's okay'; While it is a joke, therapy people will sometimes respond affably, and make a major exception; This is precisely the kind of behavior that defines recovery from seasonalism or seasonal affective disorder: not just a mere form of behavior, but a painfully specific pattern of social mood modulation; Thus, it makes sense that in the most serious cases what is presented is an immunity to that type of modulation; Another obvious answer is

263

that the response is a response to climate
and only climate, in which case suspicions
would be confirmed that a person needs
better material means, such as a space
heater or more blankets; If that is not the
case, then there must be a problem with
modulation such as the earlier social mood
modulation, or else a potentially similar romantic modulation problem; If there is a
potential in treating a broad variety of
cases, it is because the above treatments
were effective, or because the cases key
into a similar mood, independent of its
cause::

Self-Harm -

Pessimism/ exper- imentation	Random danger
Sensitiv- ity / Rep- etition	Social tol- erance / despair

Because society is seen as an outer category, there is a unique quality of sensitive
compulsion that makes people think of suicide; They seem to believe (in a grandiose
case) that their bodies are greater than
their lives, or (in the case of an inferiority
complex) that an outer dream steals the
vital impulse of their diminished bodies; In

these two senses, the attraction may have more to do with compulsion---a compulsion for passivity in the case of grandiosity, and a compulsion for exterior importance in the case of inferiority---than it has to do with genuine despair; For example, schizophrenics who happen not to be depressed have an odd kind of frenetic activity, but are much less socially involved; This may express a sense of physical realism, but also isolation, in the case of the non-depressed person; Part of this may suggest less proneness to risk; Risk seems like a physical thing to those who conduct self-harm, whereas it seems radically abstract, even superstitious, to the mentally ill who do not self-harm; In so-called ordinary cases, self-harm is a response to real-life events which have assumed dangerous importance, reflecting a similar relationship between concepts of materialism (e.g. determinism) and proneness to risky behavior; The person is often weighing the risks of someone's reprisal, or real symptoms of loneliness or purposelessness which must be overcome::

Semblancy as Precondition - Structurally, functionally, consciousness depends on a particular precondition; Independent of any mind-body theory of identity (and I think most if not all theories are variations on this), there is a particular original state of semblance which distinguishes between the conscious and unconscious, the known

and unknown states of matter; Although
this may seem like a narrow gap, it exists
in multiple forms which may occur repeatedly, and with complex association, in turn
affecting the very structure of the process;
For example, grammaticians have distinguished between resemblance and as-
semblance; In the first state something is
unclear, or becomes clear, in the second
form something is partially or wholly functional; Therefore, I think the clearest distinction in forms of semblancy is in differences of function; Functionism becomes
the groundwork for considering the gradu-
ated boundary between necessary and incomplete semblance versus functional but
unnecessary forms of semblance, which
are meaninglessly distinguished from
higher functions; See Appendix (Role of
Semblance and Other Functions) for further reference::

Semi-Types (also called Rational Semi-
Types) Study of-

Ambiantics (a semi-type): A concept of re-
ducibility to feelings; For example, a psychological synergy that space is abstract,
and abstraction depends on sensation for
reference; Thus the idea that space is sen-
sational, that sensory dynamics determines rational physics via menta, and that
sensations can build real structures;

Arbivocation (a semi-type): The employ-ability of the job search, amounting to arbi-tration of abstraction or projects ('ends') by parallel or serial processing to equal a figurative 'anteroom utility'; This utility, while descriptive of all potential jobs, is not always treated as the central utility; There is an argument from efficiency that arbivo-cation is the only valid form of employment in an information society;

Sciensation (a semi-type): The much ig-nored rationality of sensation; Attributed to an objective argument for the mind or a relative argument for utility, what follows is the existential quanta of correspondence between the mind and experience; Essen-tially, reasons may be independent of the body, because they are always corrobora-tions with notions of authenticity; Excep-tions to this look like God or primitivism, with problems native to those disciplines;

Typephasse (a semi-type): The tendency of age to inhabit a category; (1) Life de-pends on moving death from a single cate-gory to multiple incomplete categories, (2) Categories themselves are both old and young, and it doesn't do to fixate on just one of these types: everything that is old might be better young, yet age is the scale of quantifiable advantages, (3) Individual people shouldn't fixate on one category unless the category is immortal; For the individual category is actually disposable unless it combines youth and age::

267

Sexual Epitome - Is a technical word I developed to explain a cycle of correspondences that occurs in ordinary relationships; The cycle relates to four categories, which correspond to the inner, the masculine, the feminine, and the outer; The inner part, including the semen and the orgasm and generation, respond to names, which, independent of truth, determine the level of attachment to prospective parents:

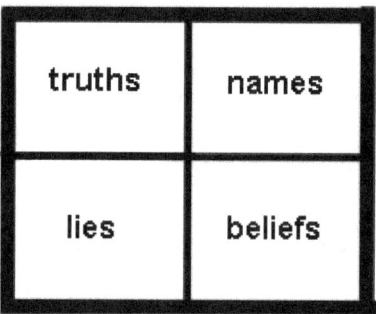

truths	names
lies	beliefs

(Diagram reads clockwise from upper r.)

Approaches may be word-intensive or word-obsessive; The male, as a function of words, is attached to truth or statedness of some kind, showing his loyalty and selfishness in how the organism appears; This is like a surface level, and names are its dimension; The third level is the feminine, dominated by lies or in female speech, fantasies, which are neither beliefs nor truths, and may or may not have a dedication to the names that have been expressed; These perform an important function in translating truth into fantasy; The fourth category is neither masculine nor feminine, and concerns belief; It is close to the feminine lie and what the masculine is most intimately concerned with; Beliefs are created by the feminine lie or fantasy, and lead back to the inner level of names; Thus, importantly, there is a metaphysical function in the realm of belief; An individual may be obsessed with one or more levels without even engaging in sex::

Sexual Predators -

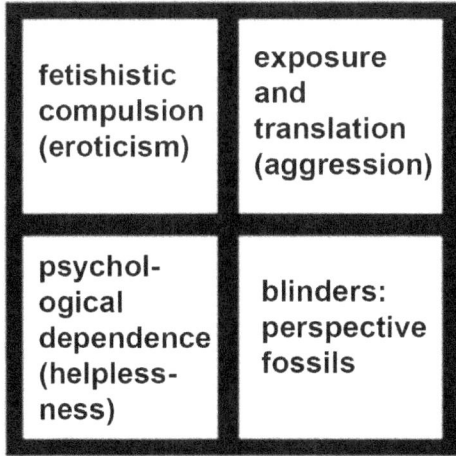

fetishistic compulsion (eroticism)	exposure and translation (aggression)
psychological dependence (helplessness)	blinders: perspective fossils

These express four general categories of

269

simple-form predators (excluding non-sexual killers) and one dynamic character of complex predators, which may be translated in whole or partial form; Attention may be paid to the psychology of interdependence that develops between the aspects of the cycle; For example, in a simple form involving only aggression, it may be that other aspects such as blindness or eroticism play a role in the conscience, specifically in relation to words like 'pervert' and 'predator', with a distinct weakness in re-envisioning the context; E.g. the criticism becomes established in the concept, re-enacting futile variations of self-identity; These become parts of the act, they become in a sense, its creativity; They become its self-reflection; Thus, even simple forms may be translations of the complex form; Study is made of the reality of categories or language in defining reality::

Sidereal Thought - The first spiritual level of cognition, corresponding to the non-physical duality, the "essence" of life, and the higher animal; Most conventionally, the sidereal concerns the vision of stars and aspects of metaphysical navigation (overcoming confusion); The higher animal is often the most dynamic aspect; It can reflect personal systems, and through them the influence of literal symbols and visions such as archetypes of progress and transition; Ultimately this is only the surface of a wider and much more wild or cosmopolitan set of correspondences such as spiritualism and other modes of thought; See also Subtil or General Thought, and Special or Universal Thought::

Simple and Non-Trivial - In the context of psychology I have attempted to turn away from the specifically philosophical com-plexities introduced in the first volume (Dimensional Encyclopedia Vol. I); But in doing so, there is a typical double-fold; First, we are not asking if philosophy or logic in general is trivial; Second, we are not asking if the psychology is trivial; Thirdly, the client's individual philosophy or logic may be trivial, but his or her psychol-ogy is not trivial; Fourthly, while the psy-chology may reduce to the non-trivial, it may also reduce to a non-trivial philosophy or logic; Fifthly, it may be determined if the logic or philosophy is psychological in na-ture, and if it may still be non-trivial infor-mation; Efforts have been made toward so-called trivial psychology, most notably Carl Rogers' efforts at client-oriented ther-apy; However, there is still a danger that the client would see him or herself as a trivial subject; This 'paradox' comes about because of the complexities of psychology; The client may be overwhelmed with the formalities of psychology, and not feel like an integral subject; He or she may feel that 'It could as easily be someone else'; The client can be reassured that she or he is non-trivial, even when the subject is simple to the psychologist; That way professionalism is compatible with the client's sense of justice; The client can be reassured that there is 'Always some level' that is interesting, and that that interest is a professional interest, and not a personal one; Another value of the non-trivial is the non-trivial quality of the trivial itself; One may ask, for example 'Has anyone ever remarked that you are covered in fuzzies?' (or some other, more relevant insight); Although trivial in nature, it is often these types of statements which give significance in the neurotic mind (and hence also to the functional mind), and thus there is a potential to combat triviality; It is precisely at this point of neutral judgment that the patient has potential to make lucid insight about him or herself; It can be stated that 'I only meant when you actually were covered in fuzzies, of course'; This brings a sense of non-triviality to a trivial subject, bringing insight into that central category called normalcy; By relating to the non-trivial, the client is also discovering the value of the trivial; That is how it translates to the psychologist::

Social Personality - An initial context may be formulated on the basis of four categories:

unknown identity	popular idea
resolving impress- ions	tradition- al attitude

Each of the four category sub-divides into four additional categories:

Popular idea:

success- ful	parad- igmatic
opinion- ated	un- popular

Unknown Identity:

enjoyer (present)	anticip-ator (future)
rememb-erer (past)	determ-inist (fate)

Resolving Impressions:

directed	trail blazer
recept-ive	confused

Traditional Attitude:

celeb-rator	priest
drifter	passive

Cont'd.

The four charts divide into four primary social personalities:

I. *Socialite:* Paradigmatic enjoyer, receptive to passivity;

II. *Psychic:* Successful rememberer, confused about priests;

III. *Colleague:* Opinionated determinist, trail-blazer and celebrator;

IV. *Artist:* Unpopular anticipator, directed drifter;

Since each of these consists of entirely different labels, personalities can be rated as resembling one or another type, in percentages;

Notice that each type has a problem; The Colleague may think others are better than him, the Artist is the worst type, but also seems to know what's going on; the psychic has a complex life, because of superior memory; the socialite has the most to offer, but may be less self-serving than others predict; In this way, all the types are off-balance::

Social Psychology - should be separated from the bitter seed that it appears to be; Instances for example in addictive psychology and mass psycho-sexual psychology may be abbreviated as a response to neediness that may exist without the dramatic stimulus; Then it is important to note that nonetheless individual responses may be a form of social psychology in the sense of informing larger social impetuses, either through unexpectedly strong influence, or through conformity; The effect is that there is no ignoring that addiction and sex play a role in the root nature of psychology, even when they are isolated instances in the total population; Essentially, mass psychology is a product of available symbols, which may interplay with the minimum prevalent role of pleasure and action as reflections of inherently-held properties of individuals; The greatest confusion then occurs when individuals are themselves major properties of society, creating 'stratified response' that may favor some actions or pleasures over others' consensus symbols; Adding to this is the prevalence of confusion in informing social decisions; To some degree, the authority of agreement exists as an illusion if it is not actually emotional knowledge which informs a decision, or if conversely the decision process does not itself connote emotion; One alternative that is widely accepted amongst professionals is that emotion is a secondary attribute; But if emotions do not have authoritative influence one may question the validity of an emotional standpoint on life, creating critical difficulties; In the context of social psychology, this seeming inability to receive con-

fusion, either by rejecting emotional authority or by emotionalizing a decision
seems to perform a selection in which
ideas become emotions which are unregu-
lated by context; This is further confused
when it is decided that it is some sort of
deeper, more dangerous influence which
shapes social psychology, and not ideas at
all, leading to a three-stage separation between emotions, ideas, and context;
(Ultimately the decision to include individuals as influences in the society is an important one, since the idea of society as a
function of brutal facts relies on individuals
for its idea; Still, in a synthetic context one
could believe that individuals are not influences, but this has the effect of questioning the existence of society); Resolving
this separation often involves a kind of un-
balance, for example, individualizing, intel-
lectualizing, or contextualizing society,
something that seems to create an excessive degree of technicalism and ultimately
by eliminating important correspondences
between the areas; In a coherent view, the
decision is to brand any aspect of psychological function in parallel with some brand
of social function; This has the potential to
alienate some intellectual factors if these
are not themselves 'understood' in a social
context; Who are we to say for example,
that all functional citizens are intellectual
citizens, or all functional social psycholo-
gies benefit from ideas?; Perhaps intellect
(the word) is only a 'thorn' that prevents
genuine feeling; (Conversely, how do we

277

function without a controlling intellect?); At a time when robotics is becoming prevalent in the minds of many people, there is a new form of alienated quality, that social psychology may not be the under-riding mechanism afterall; But this is not the feeling when social psychology seems to be a function of problems, and when the solution, more often than not, is individual, in spite of illusions::

Social Psychology Thesis - People are organized by drugs; This is much as early hunter-gatherer women were psychologically segregated if they ate certain berries; This is why eating berries is such a strong symbol in society, because it serves to organize other foods and drugs; The organization of drugs then becomes an implicit arbiter of identity; The early animist conception that a drug could have the life of a person has been fossilized in the idea that drugs themselves *are* identities; As wine drinkers were said to be 'wild and free', sugar now says that people are 'sweet', a nomengelt for conformity; The obvious or suppressed function of individual drugs or medicines also associates with other drugs, creating patterns of organization and disorganization, perhaps depending radically on perspective and subsistency; Drugs are often used to allay guilt, to participate in what might be called 'social conscience'; The psychic effect is to spread the guilt and make crimes seem ambiguous, even to conceal the existence of a problem under an umbrella of complexities masked by superficial good feeling; People come to represent masks, a reflection of the power of theatre and drama---the 'obvious effect' or affectation; Some people, when they decide that it is the sweetness in life that counts, or 'wine with good company', they invert their true desires with the apparent fulfillment of that object, creating a mask; That is not to say that the individual who does not take drugs isn't participating in social psychology---for there is a new role for authentic history (personal systems) in arbitrating what has become an obviously alienated----a chemically segregated society; These systems anchor in nature, providing proof of laws more inviolate than the flux of society; Paths of reasoning provide a manner of arbitrating that social reality is not one of only chemistry, but also of 'characters' and 'properties' which are not individual or selective; If the complexity of chemistry proves too daunting, there is an entic caveat in which drugs may prey on one another for reinforced significance; The authentic and 'clean' individual becomes the natural interlocutor for alienated species of people who would otherwise cease to communicate; Any formal pattern of functional existence must be sheerly beyond the chemical muddle, raising the prospect that functions are formalities, and beyond the realm of chemical testing lies a realm

279

of chemical truths; Generally, to affirm the theme of a chemical thesis is also to confirm that this is a social thesis, rather than a mere exercise in Zen; For the complexity of chemical association is inextricably bound to the psychosomatic pattern of the entire history or subtext of stimulation, namely the complexity of experience; The complexity of stimulation is also the hieratic relation to other members of society, and the recognition of disrelations, which frequently figure in the iconization of egoism.

SOCIAL PSYCHOLOGICAL THEORIES

Realization - Integration - Constructivism

Primitivism - Adaptation - Noesis

Recognition - Supplementation - Judgment

Pre-Cognition - Mimetics - Post-Cognition

Definitivism - Exceptionalism - Variativism

Embodied Cognition - Synthesization - Behaviorism

Statics - Co-Variation - Evolution

Mechanism - Biology - Spirituality

Trait Theory - Interactionism - Situationism

Development - Selection - Dynamics

Knowledge - Potential - Learning

Objectivism - Thematics - Perspectivism

Complexivism - Conditioning - Reductivism

Social Stratification Operators - Responses to 'We prefer our own perspective to have privileges':

[But] 'They like us': This is a primitive level that gives in to egalitarianism and then complexivism and exceptionism; With that said, it can be complex within a certain level of commitment;

[But] 'They are our representatives': Motivated by self-interest, others' privileges may be preferred out of an assumption in their advantage; When (if) it becomes obvious that one's own privileges are denied, then there are two choices: (A) Formalizing others' privileges into a 'social system' or (B) Adopting a flexible concept of privileges;

[But] 'They are deep': Between the two preceding answers [A and B in 'representations'] there is a paradigm to psychologize the opposition; For otherwise there is a brutal 'enigma' to contend with that cannot be understood in simple terms, a 'relatively insane agent of agendos'; If the privileged are deep, this enforces a Pavlovian paradigm for 'anticipated rewards'; But the result is a contrast with personal value; The choice at this stage is to increment the criterion of judgment resulting in 'they have the crystal' or to find a psychological balance in what looks like a

282

reciprocal relationship at a juncture of dis-
advantage; Someone could choose one of
several things without incrementing judgment: [A] Find constant rewards in life, [B]
Relate with only the underprivileged, [C]
Assume constant progress or irrationalism;
The general fault is in the communication
of privilege which might still be 'some secret';

[But] 'They have the crystal': This method
of selecting a preferred object has deep
implications, such as in the inflection of a
kind of contingency or synthetics to the
proposition of status or authority; Although
the system appears synthetic, it is at this
point when it rests on its firmest ground as
per unconscious reinforcement; But this
has side effects that may affect addiction
disorders: the assumption of the prevalence of a social paradigm or 'mode of cachet' does not under-ride all social modali-
ties with the same type of credibility; In
some cases the unconscious authority is
prevalent, but without the same reasonable social utility, as in addictions; Alternately, some forms of social stratification
may treat the addict like an object, in
which case the addiction confers an exclusive form of social authority; But with exceptional exceptions come exceptional
problems which may be optimal for a mythology of products; However, this system
leaves the superficial majority (of commitments) feeling like victims of abuse, just as
the term 'drug abuse' implies; And the al-

ternative to 'living on the surface' may well be too much of a compromise; The result is a kind of 'consumerism for the gods' in which all real consumers are said to be privileged, and in most cases sacrifice key advantages for a piece of the 'parlez faire'; The concept of 'mode of cachet' has reached into media streams such as Anime cartoons, showing how even this furthest level of stratification participates with the baseline consumer, in a potential cycle of re-process; This determines that there are several areas of consumerism which receive differing privileges, based upon differing information: [A] The decidable or committed consumer, [B] The luxury consumer, [C] The participatory consumer, and [D] The helpless consumer; Usually although the stages represent increasing levels of neuroticism vis. the advertising, the fourth stage relatively has the most to gain by the product, whereas the first has the least; [Advertizers then give the luxury consumer 'quality random' information with the hopes of convincing them that they are not subject to the same forms of psychological research; While in another respect they may be the 'most processed' consumers behaviorally]; This study anticipates the growing meaninglessness of what it means to be a 'recreational drug'::

Softness - is a trend in the psychological turn on philosophy; Essentially, logic may imply emotions when it implies cognition, and also understanding emotions may be required for understanding values; In this second respect psychology may also be undergoing a philosophical turn, in that it is beginning to seem possible to map emotions and organize them, although it has been discovered that emotional conditions are highly exceptional, and thus have highly specific properties, even when categories of function are generalistic; One promising aspect of this is the quasi-universalism or minimal understandability of interface responses, particularly when preferences are taken into account; Interfacing with emotions and thoughts promises to reward those whose preferences have been mapped into such a system; The question is, must psychology take a hard line on the growing number of disorders in the context of preference-logic? Perhaps a soft approach would be more rewarding for those who are just looking for simple bottom-up benefits like recognition, artificial empathy, or a self-serving merit system; (It turns out, these may encompass a large area of interactions); In the future, there is some margin of acceptance for soft approaches.

Sophisticated Words - like liaison, lar-
ceny, and protectorate have potential to
blur psychology in the convention of Eng-
lish; These words may require a particular
brand of social understanding that is only
available to select professionals; Further,
even the professionals themselves might
not understand the nuances of the words
that are being used: words may have un-
dertones of slavery, hermetic learning
such as morality or legal conventions, and
certain assumptions about behavior which
may be dated and provide no obvious
guide points for those outside the specific
legal, moral, or professional system; Adding to the problem is the fact that most if
not all of these conventions are not obviously psychological in nature, creating a
sensitivity and even a knowledge problem;
In the case of the word liaison used widely
in government, there is a sense of purpose
bound uniquely with government that has
military overtones; Consequently, individuals may find an unreasonable desire to be
violent resting in the back of their minds;
This sensation may only be exacerbated
when government is perceived to have the
authority to present its own coherent mental structure; Individuals are then forced to
adopt a blind mentality in which violence
specifically is a force delegated to government (according to convention); This force
may then appear uncontrollable, creating
problems when the psyche can influence
government; The consequent action is to

286

instate what appears to be a soulless government, with some serious consequences; But alternately, the effect may be one of perception, only affecting uneducated groups; Again, this affirms the earlier principle that sophisticated words are not always understood; For example, if abstraction is the largest problem, there is a secondary problem of development, a period during which there is a lapse in understanding; By the time some understand the words they are using, they may be locked into the system; Thus, the response to sophisticated words involves some psychic power.

Special or Universal Thought - The third level of spiritual cognition, associated most consistently with saints, bodhisatvas, and yogis; This involves a certain degree of unattachment from life, which some associate with a spiritual decree or contract from purposefulness and preservation; The special insight may be personal and at the same time social relevant; The universal may be insignificant and at the same time all-enveloping; Special insights have sometimes extended the aphorism and mathematics; Universal insights have sometimes extended the metaphorical and pedantic; These modes are often associated with a strict formulation of life; Nonetheless, some may go beyond this, and many are aware of it; See also Sidereal Thought and Subtil or General Thought::

Squirrel Realities - Some people have questioned if their inner resources are in some way stolen, or if there is some artificial way where our emotions are a product of some kind of mechanical accounting book; Certainly emotions vary, but there is no need to affirm an outer sacrifice of our inner resources to support the view that there is some kind of sacrifice which occurs for us individually; Consider that for the purposes of proof, there is no meaningful difference between individual sacrifice and sacrifice arbitrated by a second or third party (such sacrifice is just or unjust, desirable or undesirable, independent of other people); Therefore, there is no meaningful difference in whether these inner resources are acquired by some local biological process, or instead some noospherical balancing book; The effect could look the same if we assume that functional people are sane; So there is a further bailiwick: there is no reason to believe that 'squirreling' is fake, because the difference is meaningless::

Stimulation, Authentic - Posit that there are feelings other than happiness of equal importance: then stimulation is authentic when it has four properties:

assoc. memory	psychic presence
emotional impression	integral/ authentic meaning

These may be seen as more dependent on general sensitivity, and less dependent on stimulation for ultimate significance, than is traditionally realized; See also Collective Unconscious::

Stress Response -

STRESS THREAT RESPONSES: PROBABILITY

CHANCE OF HAVING NO PROBLEM: DETERMINED BY CONTEXT

CHANCE OF ADEQUATELY DEALING WITH SOME FORMS OF STRESS: 100%

CHANCE OF ENCOUNTERING EXTREME FORMS OF STRESS
(AT SOME POINT):   100%

CHANCE OF ADEQUATELY DEALING WITH EXTREME FORMS OF STRESS: 50%

CHANCE OF BEING BIOCHEMICALLY DAMAGED BY STRESS: UNDETERMINED

Some of these statements follow from a relativist position in which, for example, in a calm and relaxed life small forms of stress seem like extreme forms of stress; Virtually, this is linguistically truthful for that

type of condition; So I conclude that relaxation indicates better response to stress
(better cognition) but oftentimes less rational judgment of what stress entails; Arguably, however, this is only because
more extreme forms of stress activate survival mechanisms; Just as they do so, the
more relaxed state activates mechanisms
which serve the advantage of that state of
finding relaxation; So stress has no ultimate advantage, except survival, so long
as it does not serve the defense of greater
or lesser forms of stress response.

Subtil or General Thought - The second
spiritual level of cognition, often involves
insights or 'impressations' about signs or
aspects of the world or personal observa-
tions; In this sense it may be more visionary than Sidereal Thought; Via modes of
reasoning, the subtil insight can relate between intelligence and wisdom, or elaborate on the beauty or desolation of life; Alternately, the general insight can find a
universal significance for a single object,
or interpret an entire series of events as a
work of genius; The subtil can be aphoristic or mathematical, and the general can
be metaphorical or pedantic; See also Sidereal Thought and Special or Universal
Thought.

Sugared Words - Usage that may come under prejudice from paranoid patients, but which should be considered carefully; The schizophrenic does not want a false vision of life, but at the same time he or she may not find the sweetness of the ordinary very appealing; So what he or she means by "sugared words" is entirely different from the therapist; The schizophrenic may be very open to comparing (real, preferred) sugared words to science fiction, whereas the therapist may be resigned to a more clinical subscription; The schizophrenic may not find reassurance in any reference to the clinical context, however subtly it is guised in politeness or personal references; This important difference (between the patient and the therapist) is one of the foundations for the Extra-Categorical Theory of Schizophrenia.

Superbal Information - The study of psychology which is determined by the existence of the soul or non-corporeal body, or even the interpretation of life as a kind of suspended dream-state, may also be determined in regard to subtle or 'superbal' information, which is interrelated with concepts of psychic prediction and intuitionism; Typically, the gathering of such information depends on an almost invisible layer of reality, a reality which exists on the surface of all things; In one sense this layer could be called 'information' while in another sense it is clear enough that it cannot be gathered without considerable skill; However, it does not involve a psychic technique in the sense of having a causal relation to a subject, or a special humanistic interpretive function; Instead, all subjects are largely treated as the same; The simplest approach is the psychic technique of honesty, which provides a direct bridge between the observer and the subject; Additional strategy may be had by eliminating confusions and obtrusions which interlude between the material that is observed and the psyche of the observer; There is an initial danger that the content of the subject and the meaning of the observer is distinctly unrelated, that no meaning could be found in the material; For this purpose, an additional layer of honesty is required, a kind of 'honest significance'; The result, without skill, is a kind of subjective connotation; Effort must then be taken to translate between the subjective and the objective; Several alternatives to that form of un-determination present themselves; In one technique, perspective is gained on the 'entire subject' including subjects which enclose the observer; In this way, a direct link is established between the significance of the observer and the significance of the subject or material; 'How would the observed phenomena answer questions, and how do these question relate to me?' can be asked; This may be related to the techniques of Psychic Prediction; A further level of this is to interpret how the meaning

292

for the observer translates again back into the significance of the subject; The emphasis should be on some significance that is not quotidian; Another technique is to interpret how the 'smallness' of the subject relates to the 'largeness' of general reality, resulting in some statement of general significance; A more skilled version of this is to interpret the 'language' of the subject or material, as a reference to the 'language' of the larger world or reality; If there is an exceptional way to organize language, the organization of language can be used to find a 'location' for a subject amongst all subjects; A final technique, which is especially desirable, is to interpret a subject's 'location' directly, for the purposes of deriving representative statements; This technique takes the utmost intuition, and should be practiced repeatedly on everyday subjects and materials for experience.

Suppression Techniques - have been used in light of some disastrous cases in using Freudian re-immersion, usually in conjunction with medication; These techniques, because they are not the primary treatment in extreme cases, are termed "light" techniques; But one should not underestimate the importance of their principle, particularly when individuals who are prone to overstating their case are at risk also of obfuscating the core components of their mind or pathology; This is evident

most archetypally in the cases of hypochondriacs and highly successful people;
In these cases the specialized importance
of details and conditionalities really reduces to an immaterial cloud of supposition; The expressed objections and pos-
tures are really a work of imagination, because there is no problem to treat; The
therapist is given two alternatives: to intel-
lectualize the problem so that it seems interesting, or to convince the patient that he
is being ridiculous; Largely, and abversely,
the role to inducing suppression is to convince the patient that he *is* a hypochon-
driac or *is* being successful; A secondary
technique is to partially recover
(conditionally recover) concepts or experiences which are recognized as irrational,
depressing, etc.; The secondary conditioning serves as a context-of-reference for
realizing success; See also Recovery
Techniques.

Symbolism -

Interpreting Symbols in Daily Life

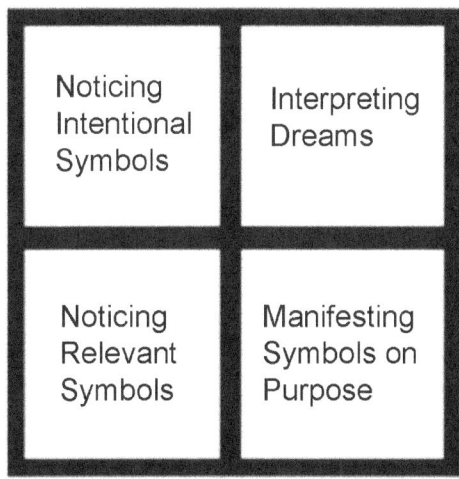

Diagram reads C.C. from upper right
::

Szasz, Thomas - Controversial theories concerning the non-physical origin of mental disease have been widely supported in a therapy setting by reference to the context of the psyche and the unconscious; However, Szasz brings an additional component that social influences are the most formative for mental health and development; For example, influences such as verbal and attitudinal cues may affect place of living, specific choices (if any) about work environment, etc. The deep implication is that volitional forces which are treated as the vast output of cognitive wellness are largely an input of the vast social influences which largely make up the context of development; This one-two relationship is not easily changed, but must be understood in its own terms; If there is a physical component of health, it may be difficult to understand when mental factors are clearly significant indicators of environmental response; If they are not understood conditionally, they fail to be social indicators, and so they fail to be mental variables::

===============T===============

Tangential Happiness - My major theory of happiness. Happiness is 'on vacation' from the consideration of problems. This shows how happiness is a completely different mind-set, which must be married with factors like philosophy and desire-fulfillment. The byproducts largely are a casualness about realism (in philosophy), and an ability to tie practical matters to what we actually want, therefore fulfilling realism. Tangential happiness should be distinguished from unhealthy denial. I think more of these cases are actually 'conscious denial' than people commonly admit. Tangential happiness can be perceived in terms of an adventure mentality. Parsing the adventure is a way of parsing happiness. The more happiness is understood, the easier it becomes to attain it. For example, if the object of the adventure is to attain an object of desire, then happiness should be tied to the type of realism that is related to the attainability of that object. If the object is to meet a friend, the type of realism might be 'serendipity'. If the object is to write a poem, the type of realism might be 'fantastic'. By using terms that relate to happiness, the only danger is rejecting the tangential reality of happiness. This is not a method for extreme happiness, but may be used to achieve moderate contentment, also called 'functional happiness'.

Technical Choice Fallacy - The distinguishment between the sad and the content, if it can be discerned subjectively or otherwise, depends on some critical difference, a moment of critical articulation in which a resulting feeling is produced. I think particularly of the sound of urination. To one person it may seem upsetting, jarring, or distasteful, whereas to another person it may seem ebullient, reassuring, and cheerful. If the upsetting aspect is in fact a negative emotion (sometimes it may not be, for instance, if it feels fully justified to the individual), then the rational thing to do is to persuade the opposite feeling, even artificially. It becomes fallacious to perceive the urination, or any other perception, in a negative light, because such negative feelings imply thoughts or emotions which have not been justified by the mind.

Tempo - is a good concept for functional and dysfunctional types alike; While there are cases where the suggestion can be confused with a need for impulsivity¾cases in which there may already be such a problem¾largely tempo has the potential to enlarge the mental sphere and relieve stress; Tempo is also a good function for stimulating organization and general structured thinking; If a client has already dipped repeatedly in psychological jargon, a more complicated approach may be needed, such as 'relieving the tempo' or by using guided imagery; Tempo may be a theme with ironic imputations in nervous disorders, a potential source of humor, but generally affects moods in a positive and productive way::

The psychologist tries to avoid what may be called a **Token Encounter** - a situation which is too typical to connote personality; Instances with highly frustrated or guilt-ridden clients sometimes seem like more theory than fact, isolating the therapist within his or her own internal frame of reference; The solution to this may be to introduce some emotional variable to question the artificial placidity and de-motivatedness of the client's perspective; When this works, the client gains trust; At that point, the health of the client may depend on the health of the psychologist's theoretical framework; One should not for example, instruct someone who has been psychotic that all his inner conflicts are rooted in an Oedipal complex; His instinctiveness will make him think that the therapist can rationalize harm to his family; Other instances of token conflicts are also imaginable, for example, someone who obviously does not want to talk about drug possession; Someone such as this is more likely to respond to superstitious forces than an authority which could be confused with 'the system' or more dangerously, their own concept of what is wrong with themselves::

299

Training - The motive-impulse
(hypothesis) to attribute a single unexplainable trauma or a series of unexplainable traumas, to a single explicable event;
The unified event serves as a symbol
which is not always completely real; For
example, by a process called deference, a
recurrent dream about a shark attack is
not the source of trauma (assuming, that
is, that no shark attack occurred), but instead itself an explanation of other traumatic conditions; The recurrency of the
dream becomes a mnemonic for the multiple sources of trauma; As soon as secondary traumas can be found, it can sometimes be concluded that these too are high
-level symbols for *aversions to harm*; Symbols for aversion play a strong role in the
symbolism, such as survival, love, and
medicine; This is why recovering (often
subtle) dreams of taking medicine, receiving love, or surviving alone can be particularly life-changing; However, the patient is
not likely to understand them without referring to present trauma or desire; Aversion
to harm provides a connective to the present patient, which can be understood in
terms of not an aversion, but a *desire for
meaning* within dreams; Training is in one
sense the pleasurable collection of meaning from life events, and in another sense,
the painful recovery of life events from
meaning::

Transcepsis [not ascepsis]- If someone just takes a quick time to re-think or turn around, the entire thought or mood may be different; This has a kind of token value in describing the constancy (or conversely, the inconsistency) of symptoms of mental illness; Perhaps the patient is over-committed to his or her symptoms, or playing the role of an (even un-willing) hypo-chondriac; Sometimes this same problem affects patients who are well-treated; Perhaps, if dysfunctional, they could be more functional; But if they are functional, it is possible they are using "tunnel vision" and need clarity instead; These kinds of alternatives demonstrate the use of transcepsis.

Trauma - Adequate Responses

	spoil, rancor, trauma	mal-conduction, delayed messages	suppression, hindrances, restraints
sexual	coping	education	discovery
emotional	developing	transformation	honesty
intellectual	realizing	extension	exhibition

These suggestions of course don't displace the need to get help when matters are serious; They merely point towards the functional side of what may otherwise seem unresolved psychologically.

=============U=================

Understanding Genius -
Defined as extreme intelligence.

logic/ int-entionality/ intensionality	access/ modality/ modularity
process/ sub-stantiation/ substitution	continuity/ system/ symbol

::

Understanding Intelligence -
Defined as balanced reason; Other-wise, see 'genius' or 'madness'.

Doctor-ing	Humility
Prodigy	Patience

::

Understanding Madness -

Smoothe	Dull
Sharp	Madness

::

Underworld Theory - Theory prevalent amongst both functional and dysfunctional people, characterized by superstition about large categories of reality; These categories may range from war zones, to foreign nations, to hospitals---but in the psychotic or altered state of conscious- ness may include nearby places such as a bedroom or basement; In children, varia- tions of this syndrome are typically excus- able for lack of knowledge, combined with a potential intimidation by the size of adults, and in the case of children problem areas frequently disappear during daylight- --the modern source of the mythology about nightmares; The difference is fre- quently company, knowledge, familiarity, and the level of paranoia or in the long term (such as without knowledge, com- pany, or familiarity), basic fear, either an absence of reassurance, or a presence of obsession with negativity; In some cases, fears are emergent from career or romantic circumstances::

Unitarian, The (Psychological Concept) - For most dysfunctional people, the Unitarian is a fairly high-minded concept. In the same way that the committed Disintegral strives to become an Amalgam, so-too, the Amalgam seeks to become the Unitarian, and the Unitarian seeks to become the Integrator. The Unitarian is an integrated form of the Amalgam. The Unitarian has ideas the Amalgam did not have, and these ideas tend to be functional and serve to benefit the person in his or her life. The Unitarian becomes predictable and reliable. The ideas are not always original---often they are borrowed from the tradition of good ideas which has come before this person. That is the usual Unitarian realization, that a functional concept can be borrowed for personal benefit. Occasionally (very rarely) there is someone who jumps directly from the Amalgam to the Integrator, by integrating an original function in society. However, most of the time, there are many fragments of realization before the entire Unity is realized. For functional people, this occurs during childhood, sometimes very early. But for many other people, Unity may occur late in life, or not at all. It is worth emphasizing that the Unitarian is the natural development of

the Amalgam, although it requires significant achievements which are well beyond
what is possible some of the time. The
Unitarian is an exceptional Amalgam, the
way the Integrator is an exceptional Unitarian::

Vis. **Universal Psychology,** human motivations are theorized as to always fall under some psychological explanation; With
divinity or a noosphere it is theorized that
all physical things can additionally be explained as aspects of thought or motivation; Without divinity or a noosphere, it is
thought that everything might be explained
irrationally; With reason, there is seen to
be a choice, at least amongst the opposites of those categories, namely, no mind,
no matter, and the presence of gods; This
becomes a thoroughgoing theory of the
conditional reality of the human mind::

Unlocated Disorder - Disorders which refer to no real location; These occur especially in the era of video games and virtual
reality; The problems often develop by fix-
ating upon an artificial object or perception
that has no real-world spatial location; The
object or perception becomes fossilized in
the mind, or in some quasi-mental or personal space, both less real than an obsession and equally persistent; Unlocated disorders of the genuine fantasy variety are
becoming less common; More often than

not the problem is the result of self-imposed repetitive behavior such as video games, television, or masturbation, which leaves a visual 'sprite' on the mind, or some unavoidable fascination which is not interesting enough to terminate; The image, object, or perception becomes residual; Techniques of self-judgment may be used to clear the assumption of the relevancy of these partially unconscious concepts; In the worst cases the images may be the result of childhood or adult trauma, leading to associated techniques of recovery or suppression.

Untangling Thoughts -

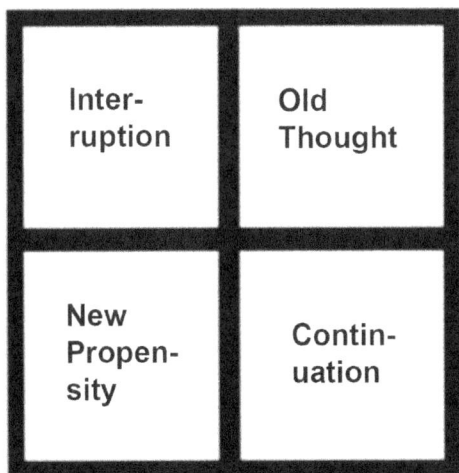

For example: (1) I hate it when the tea

doesn't strain, (2) I love it when the tea does strain, (3) I love the property of the tea when its straining, (4) I still find it lovely when / while the tea strains; It's this last type (#4) that you should keep in mind when you need patience.

==================V================

Veau Faux - While I have been reluctant to introduce French concepts into my book of psychology---France is remembered for existentialism and post-modernism, two disciplines which leave a legacy of irration- alism---one concept which seems to need addressing is the Veau Faux (voh fah-w), or false time; Veau Faux expresses the susseration of pretenses within the surface -subliminal; It affects social psychology as an irrational interruption which has inter- posed itself on otherwise rational events; It is characterized as appearing and disap- pearing like a cloud, having its own ambi- ance of confusion, and often embodying its own ideas, such as memes, tropes, or norms; It is this characteristic of a cloud- like quality which links the Veau Faux par- ticularly with time; It is argued that unless time embodies pure rationality, some irra- tional element will occasionally emerge, which will have its own identity, often inde- pendent from individuals; And so long as time is a distinct concept from rationality, time must be characterized as partly irra- tional; Thus, the Veau Faux is a very prevalent concept::

Vertedness (Introversion and Extroversion) - A diagram can be drawn like the following:

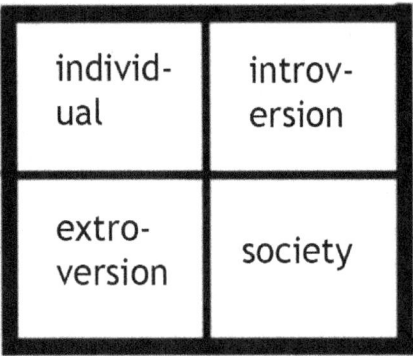

Using categorical methods, the conclusion is that either an introverted individual has an extroverted society, or an extroverted individual has an introverted society; But the comparison also functions from quantity versus singularity and other properties of the four quadrants such as emotion versus abstraction.

Singularity versus quantity serves as an argument for extroversion: If society is quantity, and individual is singularity, then singularity is introverted when quantity is extroverted; This expresses such states as the psychotic and the sexual fetish; Also in the same analysis, singularity is extroverted when quantity is introverted; This seems to express the converse, complex reality, of the so-called 'justified' extrovert;

But there is no necessity to be compelled to compare the introvert with quantities.

Another comparison, of emotion with abstraction, becomes an argument for introverts, but uses introvert and extrovert as the base properties: If introversion is abstraction, and extroversion is emotional, then individual abstraction implies an emotional society, and social abstraction implies individual emotion; The result is a defense of the conjunction of emotion and abstraction, or 'a society of individuals', ala introvertedness.

Neutral Vertedness:

The categories might be revised under the logic that intro / extro is only one-dimensional, and thus represents only one quality; It is also true that a revision is mandated by the original meaning of 'vert' meaning love or alliance.

Similarly, vertedness might be seen under the following limited classifications:

"Expressive-Abstract," and "Public-Private,"

Giving each of these terms values can show something about the capacity for learning, or the combination of factors which contribute to social functionality and private intelligence.

The 'Four Personalities in this mode are:

Expressive Public Personality
Expressive Private Personality
Abstract Public Personality, and
Abstract Private Personality.

One thing this system does not gauge is business sense and practicality. So, additionally, one might add a differentiation between realistic and idealistic ideations. This might be placed in-between the two other category choices. So, now we have:

1. Expressive realistic public personality.

2. Expressive idealistic public personality.

3. Expressive realistic private personality.

4. Expressive idealistic private personality.

5. Abstract realistic public personality.

6. Abstract idealistic public personality.

7. Abstract realistic private personality.

8. Abstract idealistic private personality.

Virtual Psychology - centers around concepts of stimulus, especially the role of chemistry and chemical significance, and the ways that chemistry may or may not be an explanation of the sublimation of mass, group, and personal psychological concepts; In my approach to this, I am primarily rhetorical; The path of chemistry *is* psychological, but it is explained by explanations, not concepts; Chemistry, more than many things, is only intellectual when it is intellectual; Thus, it cannot be said that it is conceptual unless it already embodies some concept; The references to symbolism in chemistry are notorious for their flexibility; Thus, what is established by explanation is at least, and only, explanation; The following diagram sets out the role of virtual reality (as a psychological concept, that is, prima facie a sensation) in defining chemical stimulus; Essentially, stimulus is artificial because it is universal:

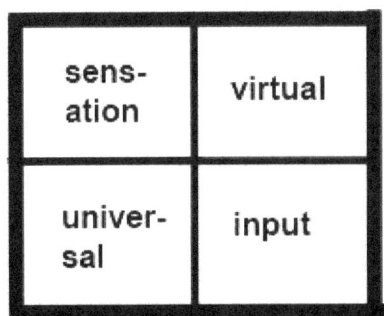

sens-ation	virtual
univer-sal	input

(Diagram reads CC from top right;)::

The Visionary Aspect - may involve connections to guiding archetypes and familiar symbols; Individuals may connect to specific ideas and references much as infants connect to specific colors as preferred elements of the spectrum; The function is not only designating a context of usefulness such as religion, techne, or memory, but also personal identification that may be influential in the behavioral development of volition and hierarchical or sub-hierarchical functioning; For example, many computer games enthusiasts will unconsciously adopt elements of their games as dominating, life-long symbolisms; Artist personalities in particular should be encouraged to sustain their visionary aspects, as there is already a deep unconscious reliance on symbolic functioning; Later encouragement may influence technical developments, or stronger relationships with family::

Volitional Difference (technical) - One of the so-called deep approaches to psychology, if it is not a matter of suppression or immersion, is to approach situations for relevant correspondence; One such method is to distinguish conditional states, and then determine if such states have psychological relevance; For example, if turning off a light makes a rat or a person secretive, then perhaps darkness is a quality of secrets in general psychological reality; Then there is an implication that a dynamic of secrets operates under darkness; (The dynamic of secrets is the psychological reality, while 'darkness' becomes a general property of psychology); The process of verification dynamic can even be extended backwards or forwards to include causation of reference (backwards), and significance or recursion of dynamic (forwards), creating degrees of reference which add truth value to most situational modes of relevance, and which incidentally resembles turning a light switch on and off; Another example is veri-fying if people think bees mean business, and if these people are related to bees or business, and then verifying how seriously that level of relevance figures in life; Per-haps the individual is 'serious about bees', or perhaps the person is 'pre-occupied with business' or perhaps irrelevant busi-ness seems more pre-occupying or seri-ous; The result is a judgment of folly, or conversely, the seriousness of activity, and can be judged modally; The result is also useful for determining if linguistic factors are responsible for a guilt complex; The effect of volition in these cases is simply that they define categories which are real space for volition::

================W=============

'Why' or 'Wowwie' - A distinction is drawn which is not precisely similar to pessimism and optimism; It is closer to honesty versus lying, but it has none of the same elements of negativity; Children may have a choice between wonder (saying 'wow') and introspection (saying 'why'); Obviously enough both forms play some sort of evolutionary advantage; Questions arise such as which one 'plays the surface'?; Perhaps 'why' is prone to materialism, whereas 'wowwie' serves values; But this ignores the greater seriousness of the 'why' question; In some respects it seems more spiritual; 'Why' may be less adapted to coping, while at the same time it is clearly a coping behavior; With 'why' there is a greater role for actual interiority, whereas with 'wowwie' there is an outer-directed sensibility that is undeniable; We shouldn't confine the issue in an assumption of polarized extrovert versus introvert thinking; Indeed, a functional introvert will probably have a potential for 'wow' reality, and a functional extrovert has a concept of 'why' although it may be remarkably different; Recently there has been a lot of criticism against 'why' favoring 'what' or 'how'; Is the difference only subjective: is 'wow' always a product of 'why'? Or is there a more complex form of development, in which 'why' means something additional? One answer is that 'why' searches for multiple answers simultaneously, whereas 'wowwie' is satisfied with one reality, however complex; Thus, the two identities express varying propensities to be manipulated by others: 'wowwie' in its simple forms, has no defense, and while 'why' is not a robust approach, it offers potential benefits in abstract knowledge, which might be gainful for society---Wowwie only benefits society through reciprocity; While it may be more wise, it is also more expensive::

===============Z===============

The Zania (or Area-of-Effect Brain) - Is a phenomenon that is considered irrational by unimaginative people, whereas creatives associate it with the rational intellect. It does exist in some form with some people, and it's meaning is clarified by concepts such as intelligence, dynamic personality, and mental cause-and-effect. The Zania is closer to being a brain than being an effect of the brain, and yet it is clear that it has outer manifestations. The Zania is known to be effected by the eating of fish and carbohydrates, and is the source of the expression that your 'Zania is growing like zinnias,' which in turn creates the expression that one's soul has been 'nourished' by something, in turn affecting expressions such as 'having a green thumb.' The Zania is the exuberant , cultivated part of the self, the part of the self reigned-in by intellect, and may lean heavily on social relationships or other ideal conditions. There is some evidence that the Zania is subject to stimulation, and may actually grow grotesquely and unpredictably in response to narcotics. This is in keeping with my Social Psychology Thesis. However, the Zania is open to other forms of nutriment as well, including sustenance such as brainfood as well as events and ideas which fascinate the person.

END

Nathan Coppedge

EXERCISES

We know that the mind is relatively functional; It merely competes with experience; Yet, we do not know that the unconscious is being functional; It may be doing supercilious things like angels dancing on the head of a pin; It may be possible to function merely as a 'function' of thinking about it; What does this bring to mind?

Think of a specific behavior; What is more important about the behavior, it's priority or its sensibility? What could change this?

What if everything were expensive, or what if everything were cheap? If everything were expensive, unless we are pessimists we might determine that everything is valuable; If everything is cheap, we might determine that everything is affordable; Discuss the matter: which is more desirable? How does this affect psychology?

What is social psychology? Is it more

likely to refer to politics or to science? Which is more desirable? Which is more false? Do you find yourself gravitating towards political or scientific descriptions of psychology? Does science offer an objective view? Is science a function of psychology? Is psychology a function of politics? Is there an objective politics? Is science a function of politics? Does psychology offer a meaningful description of either, or does it remain useful when neither is described?

Must psychology refer to a system of meaning? Must it offer a meaning of its own? Is psychology classical---or, instead, avant-garde? What is the meaning of psychology?

Nathan Coppedge

APPENDIXES

APPENDIX I. TYPOLOGIES
TWO-DIMENSIONAL TYPOLOGY

IDEAL TYPOLOGY

DIMENSIONS		
1	NATURE	: REALITY / REFERENCE
2	SOCIETY, UNCONSCIOUS	: MAJOR APPLICATIONS
3	PSYCHE, SYSTEM, SYMBOLISM (CONSCIOUSNESS) (MIND) (BODY)	: DYNAMIC REALITY
4	PERSONALITY, PERCEPTION, INTELLIGENCE, EXTENSION	: QUALIFIC REALITY

THREE-DIMENSIONAL TYPOLOGY

LEVEL 5: PERSONALITY PYRAMID

CHARACTER

FEMININE   MASCULINE

SOCIALITE   DELIBERATE   AMBITIOUS

OBSERVER   SAMPLER   ASSOCIATOR   PROCESSOR

EXPERT   CARETAKER   LABORER   SOLDIER   LEADER

LEVEL 4: DEVELOPMENT PYRAMID

EVOLVING

PRINCIPLE   SACRIFICE

SKILL   BALANCE   WHOLENESS

MOTIVATION   SUBTLETY   REPETITION   PERMANENCE

LEVEL 3: BEHAVIOR PYRAMID

INTEGRATION

INTEREST   ACTIVITY

RISK   RELIABILITY   HAPPINESS

LEVEL 2: NATURE PYRAMID

HIVE

PRIVILEGE   ADVENTURE

LEVEL 1: IMMORTAL PYRAMID

WEATHER

APPENDIX II.

BASIC PATHS IN THERAPY

Basic Paths of Therapy
for Men and Women

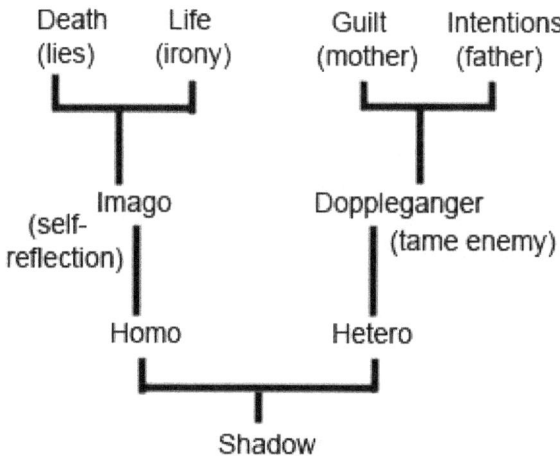

ADVANCED PATHS IN THERAPY

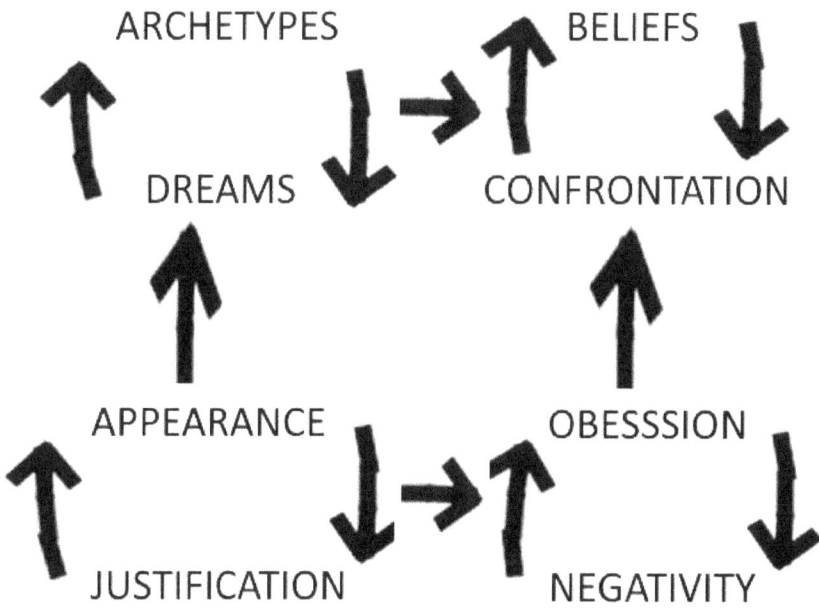

Nathan Coppedge

APPENDIX III.
DEVELOPMENT HIERARCHY

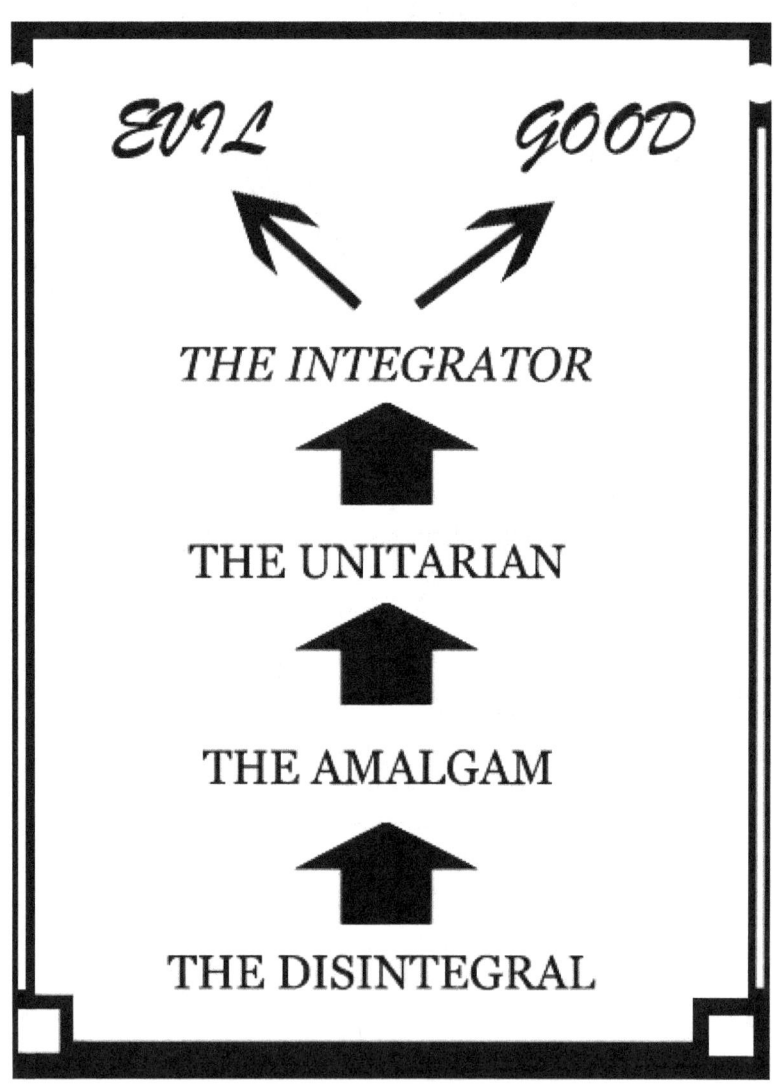

APPENDIX IV. SEX ROLES

SEX ROLES AS A FUNCTION OF HISTORY

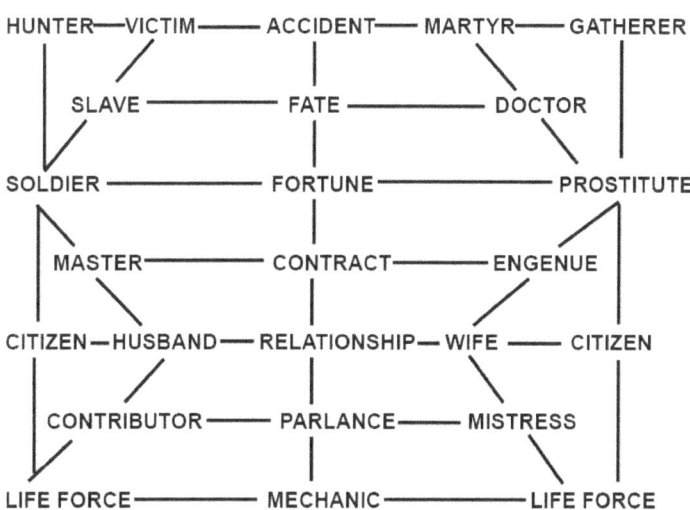

| MALE | MALE | SEX | FEMALE | FEMALE |

Homosexual variations of these involve irony such as 'purposeless doctor' and intentionally artless effete; The boundary may create a notion of the double-husband: reflecting on the concept of relationship, or in the case of heterosexuality, the double-relationship creates a 'translation' relationship of secret messages or even meaningless meaning.

APPENDIX V.
BEHAVIORAL LEMES

STATE ---> MEANING

Origin: living a lie, or living truth, or man alive, or life of atonement, etc. Lack of power, so others tend to achieve the significance. "Generous"

Infant: The more happenstantial to the parent, the more significant to the infant; spots of time, "Innocent"

Toddler: Attachment to symbols; "Crafty"

Child: Localization of complexes; "Realizing"

Teenager: Availability of information; "Processing"

Young Adult: Assumed importance; "Decision-making"

Adult: Independence; "Satisfaction"

Older Adult: Description; "Understanding"

(Post-Human): Mastery; "Comprehensiveness"

APPENDIX VI.

PRECEPTS AND MAXIMS

Behavior is affect: spatio-temporal principle;

Psychology depends on case studies, but also futuristic methods; psychology proposes new techniques just as it is receptive to the specifics of individual functioning;

If there is a fault in futurism, it is a fault that is latent in history, but not determinism, because a bad psychological theory is not a failure on the subject of history, it is a failure on the subject of individualism;

The principle of conservation is simply the validity of a present thesis (-->Research Psychology);

Open psychology is simply the psychology that rejects the rationality of fear (-->Research Psychology);

Vitality scales to the authenticity and quantity of categories present in a life (-->Contingerion);

An advantage may always be termed a generality, and a process is always selective (-->Vertedness);

333

True sadness, like all arts, to gain in truth
must gain in art (proverb)

Dimensionism, to look beyond the trivial,
must acknowledge surfaces (Conversation
with a Therapist);

The individual acknowledges authenticity,
or the individual acknowledges a lie; It is
only mystery that is complex when language is simple (Interpreting Jung);

The only hurdle in therapy is understanding (Affirmative Confirmation);

Where the patient's pessimism is opportunistic, the therapist must show that an
optimistic principle which is emergent is
not opportunistic (Fear, Basis of);

Illness is not impulsive so much as opportunistic

Part of interpretation is interpreting the in-
terpreter (Psychic Facts);

A schizophrenic may realize that immortality is dimensional dementia, and other extreme views (rational irrationalism);

It appears that one seeks to become
what one loves, perhaps even rationally (paradine of paradox);

APPENDIX VII.

MISCELLANEOUS QUOTES ON DIMENSIONAL PSYCHOLOGY

1: Dimensionism is the principle of the psyche whereby it might be quantified, even when it is qualified;

2: What denies the psychic in psychology is precisely what denies that it is a discipline;

3: The attempts at psychoanalysis are attempts at realizing the relationship between meaning and education;

4: The argument for psychology is the argument for propter hoc reality;

5: While philosophy provides a context for any caveat, psychology by working with people caveats no caveat;

6: People aren't facts is the salient truth of mathematical psychology; The distinction between fact and person creates quantity;

7: The therapist ideally should be as complex as the client, on the client's terms;

APPENDIX VIII. Thesis of Psychology

SANITY IS THE PUNT OF PERVERSITY

SANITY IS JUSTIFIED, INSANITY IS NOT JUSTIFIED

NOT A REAL CONDITION

REGARD-LESS OF CONDITION

REGARD-LESS OF CONDITION

JUSTIFIC-ATION BEHAVIOR

UNQUEST-IONED APPROVAL

PERVERSE

UNPERVERSE

SANITY IS PUNTED ON PERVERSITY

APPENDIX IX.

TRUTHS ABOUT SOCIETY AND NATURE

There is always a benefit to understanding a person; If there is no benefit, there is no understanding;

Many people work with the perspective that there should be no wrong perspective; Frequently, life raises contradictions to this fundamental presumption; If these contradictions or exceptions may be major, they may also be eccentric;

Rarely, if ever, will an organism lose the idea that it had dint in the first place; One of the terrible mysteries is how one person flourishes, while another fails from the beginning; The difference is, perhaps, experience, or merely the aptitude for success versus failure; The two aptitudes rarely seem to have anything in common; So, we see that many suffer small pitfalls where otherwise there would be an undying establishment;

Great situations, if they do not surprise and overwhelm us, have the potential to become a life-long secret of success;

What the plant does when it puts down it's roots is accomplished in the mind only

337

gradually;

Nothing prevents us from knowing the 'open mysteries' which do not subscribe to any notion of nature; Although it is difficult to substantiate their mystery, there are small evidences of the life of mystery in nearly anything; As soon as we subscribe to a mystery that is universal, we also subscribe to the genuine artifacts of nature;

APPENDIX X.

Emotional Language Techniques

1. Instead of saying "You can achieve anything you want", it may be preferred to say "You may achieve anything your heart desires", or more directly "You can achieve what you want". People appreciate direct messages, and benefit by reassurances that are not overwrought. Usually it is safe to save sophistication for intellectualism and the most intimate relationships, places where incidentally small amounts of non-sophistication can seem charming. Thus there is really no place where sophistication is appreciated, except at a distance. In close conversations the only people impressed by sophistication are teenagers. The exceptions to this are largely more emotional than factual. (There is also a relative argument that a casual approach results in sophistication. Save that angle for secondary perspectives).

2. Attachment to possessions attracts the fascination with meaning. Where one does not desire undue attention to one's personal affairs, one should not cling to the objects and antics of life in front of one's face. Instead, acting at a distance from human affairs, visualizing the real events, the innuendos and connotations of people's affairs, there is an ability to cut to the quick and avoid the hassle of being possessed by botherers and crazy-makers. If there is a danger in this approach, it is the quality of isolated thinking, and the potential follies of individuality. Although it may be more wise to entangle oneself in society the right way, isolation may be preferable to the wrong kinds of social entanglements. The objective mind in a capitalist society may seek to personalize social experiences, or else to know directly any available forms of reciprocity. Ignoring objectivity opens life to unseen eventualities, which if unfruitful, may prove to be permanent confrontations, which cannot be justified within the sense of self-purpose. Total abandon, while it may be the logic of luck, is opposed by the rational forces of individualism. There may be less of a sense of time passing to those who dwell on language and contemplation than for those that seek pleasure and inclusivity. This is the negative sense of 'time passes quickly when you're having fun'.

3. To the man, first, labor must be justified. Then labor must have results. Then labor must transform existence. Then labor must end. Labor then returns when labor is most useful. For the woman, labor is an object that is desired or not desired. Labor is an idea, which is realized or unrealized. The language of woman always promises labor, and always expresses desire. But the labor is not really desired. The labor is the undesired object, which for good reasons accompanies the more significant object, of significant persons. Woman's labor is forever unrealized, and yet makes the greatest accomplishments. Combining the two forms of labor is futile. They are near opposites. The man makes much of little. The woman makes little of much. If there is common ground between the two theories, it is the recognition of significance, either in labor, or the recognition of the great and the small, two properties which are in a confusing relationship.

4. One must 'cullinate' the ends of things to determine the path that is before one's eyes. Every sentence has an end. Every moment has a propensity. Every machine does its work. Yet everything is continually overlapping, compounding, and intermingling. One can benefit by considering that something which once stopped on someone's tongue, or which did not occur passing someone on the street, abruptly continued at a different place or time, even, ultimately, for different reasons. Life is not as abrupt as the structure of pedagogy makes it to be. Instead, abruptness is a path to continuity, to the mobilization of ideas and process-patterns which may yet stand to be imitated. Concepts---even the concept of nothing---are continuous and abrupt, in precisely the way of being objects to the mind. Indeed, the trappings of the mind have no limitation so crude as pain without adopting some precise set of rules, some unrealized potential or new propensity of purpose. Language is full of the details of others' despair, and also the sin of their thoughts. But it is through this narcosis that we have community. The emotional sense of community is realized only when abruptness ends. And yet, it may be said, abruptness is the obvious character of objects in the world. In that sense, transcendence is the law that goes un-mastered, mastering all.

APPENDIX XI. WORD-TABLE

Old Word	(New) Convention of Word
Presence	- Prescience
Meaning	- Prevalence
Proof	- Benevolence
Environment-To-Environment	- Projection
Person-to-Person	- Noesis
Stimulant	- Influence
Intellect	- Modifier

Leme - Learning habit

APPENDIX XII.

FUNCTIONS, as derived from semblance

SEMBLANCE

ASSOCIATION

PATTERNS

FUNCTIONS

LANGUAGES

IDENTITIES

WORLDS

PHILOSOPHIES

UNIVERSES

LAWS

FIGURE: The role of semblance and other functions

APPENDIX XIII.

RHETORICAL CLAIMS INTERNAL TO PSYCHOLOGY

These are rhetorical rather than medical or practical realities. They shed some light on what would ultimately be true in the ideal context of illness. While some say that that context cannot exist, it may still be reassuring in the sense that the patient can feel that it is the world, rather than themselves, that is being unrealistic. This reinforces the initial position I mention, which is that the appropriate topic for patient care is not abuse, but some more affirming set of assumptions.

The patient knows that his or her context is not meant to be a trauma, The world of the patient is not meant to be a trauma, Patient care reflects the world of the patient, Patient care must reflect a world without trauma Some claim depression is a conviction, Depression might be a symptom of a problem, But symptoms shouldn't be convicting, So depression shouldn't be a disease;

General problems affect the patient in a general way; Thus specific solutions become highly viable; Specific problems affect the patient in a specific way, so general solutions become highly viable; It is only when a general or specific solution is difficult, or when a general problem is a specific problem, that general must address general, or specific the specific; The key argument against this does not support the abstract properties of medicine, undercutting the potential for specific treatments; In fact, implementing general prevention, and general-specific prevention, if possible, could be a more powerful approach than any form of weak medicine; Thus, when the condition is relative, increasing the effectiveness of general prevention and general-specific prevention may be as effective as advances in medicine, when it is highly significant; Yet these methods are often ignored, or assumed to be implemented; Questions of preferences are sometimes ignored because the question of psychic preferences (or some other 'bizarre') theme has been ignored, the result being a lack of integration with patient realities; These realities could be accepted 'de re' without a risk of changing the beliefs of doctors; Thus there has been a 'walking on eggshells' problem, even once it is accepted that patients must be treated in a sensitive manner;

Syntactical Psychology: Rubbing the eyes is not said to contribute to blindness; Syntactical Solution: The expression 'very much' is used in a superstitious way in this context, suggesting that there is a clear solution in resolving syntax; Instead we might say 'It is possible that you have rubbed your eyes vigorously' and correlate this, if possible with poor eyesight; If there is a correlation, the reason to avoid it is only a problem of psychological syntax, not a mental disorder;

APPENDIX XIV.

PSYCHOLOGIST'S GOLD

A union of onions has no opinion
about bunions (intuit this);

APPENDIX XV.

GENIUS POTION BROMIDE

Let us propose a hypothetical potion called a Genius Potion; It grants genius, and it has no major side-effects. Given that condition, there isn't much variation in the responses amongst students:

(1) Do they always avoid it? No; (2) Would they wish for it? Obviously; (3) Would they argue against it? Only contextually; (4) Do they work for it? Maybe not (but do they like work? No);

The exceptions to the above look like the following: (1) Not thinking things through / distraction; (2) Genuine skepticism; or (3) Superstition based on real warnings;

\Testing for these last three points can be used as a complex rubric for a genius susceptibility factor; For example, if the warnings are real, then the third problem is vindicated; Thus the third answer can test reality; Skepticism can be interpreted as unintelligent when the variable involved is judged to be intelligent; Distraction can be used as a general factor of incompetence or commitment to a different variable; Thus, a creative test can ask the participant if there is something on his or her mind that is more important; That gives a quick boost to anyone being thoughtful, while rejecting unintelligent distractions; (the major exception to this last point is if there is an intelligent application that is not universally recognized as intelligent; This is also called the Pragmatic Exception);

* Screening for the earlier points screens for general intelligence and normativity; Complex responses are abnormal but intelligent, simple denials indicate a problem, or some form of reservation such as are mentioned in the second list;

* It may help to screen for honesty as a pre-test: 1. Are you a confident person?, 2. Do you like to break the rules? 3. Do you consider yourself to be honest?; To solve the quiz, confidence results in 50% dishonesty, non-confidence results in 25% dishonesty, breaking the rules results in 75% dishonesty regardless, and honesty adds 25%, dishonesty subtracts 25%. A result of zero is completely honest, a result of 75% is maximally dishonest.

Dishonesty Levels

Unconfident, good rules, honest -->0%
Confident, good rules, honest -->25%
Unconfident, good rules, dishonest -->50%
Confident, good rules, dishonest -->75%
Bad rules   -->75%

APPENDIX XVI.

CARTOONS AND JOKES
AS PSYCHOLOGY

CARTOONS: PSYCHOLOGY-AS-JOKES

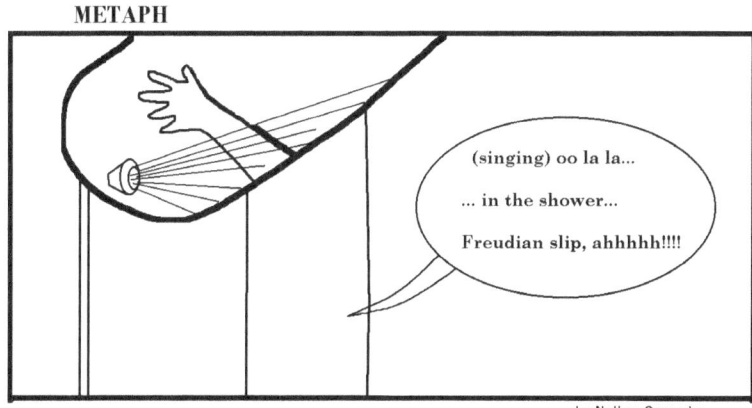

by Nathan Coppedge

AND DEATH

Archana

'ghost ship'

"goddess"

PHILOSOPHER VS WHETHER

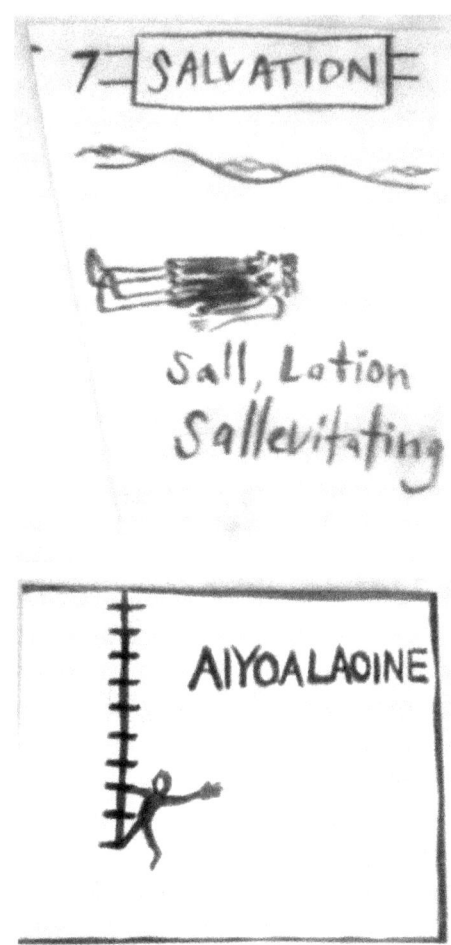

JOKES-AS-PSYCHOLOGY

Perpetual motion is a symbol of immortal life and the inventor is a god, or God invented it, or God is impossible; 'Incidental'.

The universe is one of possibility, or it is a game, or it is an endless storm; 'There seems to be equal proof of the three'.

What is preferable to women is winning an argument, or strength is preferable to women: men prefer women preferring men; 'Endless loop'.

One psychologist experiments and finds rhetoric; Another studies rhetoric, and finds experimentation; 'Methodology is a two-headed coin'.

APPENDIX XVII.

ARGUMENTS AGAINST PSYCHOLOGY

There are at least two prospective arguments against a psychological approach according to my system; One is via philosophy, and the other is via biology;

Philosophical Argument Against Psychology: Philosophy might argue from a position of logical systems, that these systems in the largest possible sense, pre-date and antiquate the formation of knowledge about the self; The philosopher argues that systemic priority antedates psychic superiority; Psychology seems to be founded on a mass exodus from systems into some kind of natural caste system; With a genuine understanding of logic, the philosopher argues, there is no caste system, instead everyone does his or her level best to find a located significance within the 'system of all systems': philosophy; If the individual does not find answers within philosophy, the answer is that she or he is insignificant;

Defense of Psychology Against Philosophy: Philosophically, psychology in the broadest sense of the word encompasses all theories of mind; In this sense, it predates philosophy organically; Philosophical systems must in some sense, depend on

357

the mind, says the psychologist; The argument that is not a function of the mind seems to lack a soul; Selfishness seems to be a stronger force than reason, and if so, perhaps more justified; The argument that justified selfishness has a soul seems more defensible than a good argument, if the argument does not have a pitch-perfect context; In this sense, psychology seems to be less difficult, and more intuitive, and qualified in both senses;

Biological Argument Against Psychology: Instead of arguing ex simpliciter that psychology isn't a system, biology argues the opposite: psychology is the most fundamental system, albeit a system too simple to explain everything; The lack of explanatory power is explained by the variety of systems that psychology is concerned with (according to biology, very few); Biology sets out to prove that multiple types of consciousness ultimately exist, using this sense of variety as a foundation for the view that psychology lacks perspective; As a function of diversity, consciousness is understood not to exist in only one form; And what could explain real differences except materialism?; The biologist excuses additional assumptions by claiming that these assumptions are based on nature rather than the mind; Although biology abandons philosophy to some extent, it also finds inspiration in some psychological concepts, such as intelligence and behavior;

Defense of Psychology Against Biology: It seems that where behavior is not a function of psychology, it almost doesn't need an explanation; And what is biology without behavior?; In this reductivist fashion, it appears that psychology is more high-minded than biology; Further, the psychologist claims that the mind is a binding concept with more universal explanatory power than physical theories which 'do not apply themselves'; The psychologist also argues that psychology is necessary to explain events which are inevitably interpreted mentally, or even to understand that perceived events have significance in the first place; Psychology is also concerned with the more direct motivations for human existence, and is therefore more apt to provide theses which correspond to immediate behaviors, environments, and the correlations of past events in history::

APPENDIX XVIII. Uncertainty Principle of Psychology:

(1) Determined or undetermined, there is no rational reason to feel defended, because defense is an artificial emotion; (2) There is no certain defense of happiness, because happiness involves defense of emotion; (3) People who are happy are defended; (4) Authentic emotions are not a defense, because they require an authentic defense; But an authentic defense cannot be absolute (change, death, etc.); Authentic emotion raises authentic questions; Thus, authentic people are gamblers; It is implied that one must ask questions, whether or not they are authentic; The exception to inquiry is a kind of unquestioning quality; One can reject facts, or one can conclude that ignorance is god, or one must ask questions; To avoid authentic questions, one cannot be authentic; (5) Happiness, sadness, or doubt, the conclusion is that matter is the brain, and it has no defense, since defense is an artificial emotion; Evidently, consciousness is a free event on real estate where there is or is not a poison; Unless life is determinate, and if it were, it would be arbitrary.

APPENDIX XIX.

Segue to Biology

A kind of negative-positive depiction

eliminated optimist	eliminated survivor
rewarded optimist	rewarded survivor

1. Eliminated survivor : eliminated optimist :: rewarded survivor : rewarded optimist

(Here the only difference is survival; innocent optimists are always eliminated, unless there is relativism)

2. Eliminated survivor : rewarded survivor :: eliminated optimist : rewarded optimist

(Here being eliminated is what deserves a reward but has nothing to do with survival---people adapt to be rewarded rather than to resist elimination)::

361

Nathan Coppedge

APPENDIX XX.

TEMPLATES

PSYCHOLOGICAL DEDUCTION

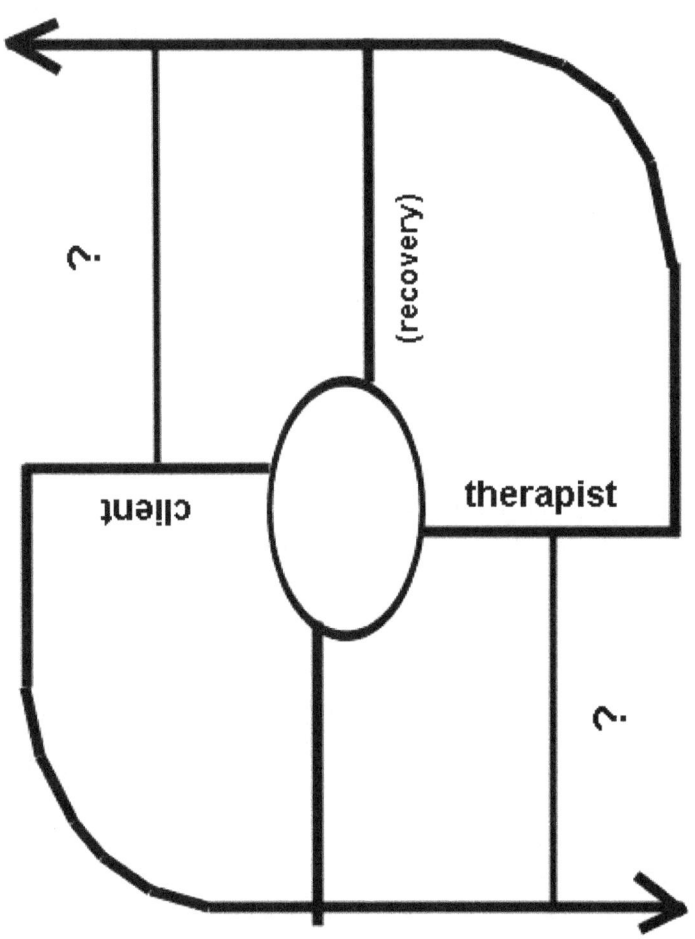

[A] Client's views are unquestioned, and the therapist's critical view is the opposite of those terms;
[B] Development of the client's is opposite of the development of the therapist's terms.

PSYCHIC PREDICTION

1.1 Ask: What is the first thing you think of?

_____

1.2 Ask: What is a related thing?

_____

2.1 Ask: What is an unrelated thing?

_____

2.2 Answer Yourself: What is the opposite of 2.1?

_____

3. Add 2.2 to 1.2. This is something meaningful to the person you asked.

LINKS

A Psychology Encyclopedia
psychology.jrank.org

All About Psychology
all-about-psychology.com

Social and Cultural Theory
cla.purdue.edu/english/theory/

Google Scholar
Scholar.google.com

Online Dream Dictionary
hyperdictionary.com/dream

Reviews of Psychology Books
metapsychology.mentalhelp.net

BIBLIOGRAPHY

Andreas, Brian. *Hearing Voices* (illustrated)

Cirlot, J.E. *A Dictionary of Symbols*

Freud, Sigmund. *The Interpretations of Dreams*

Furnham, Adrian. *50 Psychology Ideas You Really Need to Know.*

Gendler, J. Ruth. *The Book of Qualities* (creative writing)

Jung, Carl. *Man and His Symbols*

-----. *Two Essays on Analytic Psychology*

Moser-Wellman, Annette. *The Five Faces of Genius.*

Rank, Otto. *Beyond Psychology*

Stanovich, Keith. *How To Think Straight About Psychology*

Nathan Coppedge

INDEX

Nathan Coppedge

-INDEX-

[ALL CONTENTS SOURCE ALPHABETICALLY]

> →: See only under the following
>
> **See Also:**
> At category heading, see category within In-dex
> At subject description, see primary contents of the book

BELIEFS
> consistent and inconsistent (→ Dualistic Pro
> file and Deductions)

BIAS
> Channeling Objectivity
> Dishonesty
> Mood bias [→Property Paradox]
> Negative Ascription
> Perception Studies [→Noiac Studies]
> Popular Qualifier
> Pragmatic Assumption

CATEGORICAL APPROACH [See diagrams
> throughout; Also especially:]
> Typology diagrams [→Appendix I. Typolo-
> gies]
> Meaningful Praxis
> Positer Characteristics
> Social Psychology

COGNITION (See also under Psyche, Therapy)
> hidden social functions of (→Apercu)
> Mental Real Estate
> Rational Semantics

CONDITIONS
> Arachnophobia [→Fear, basis of]
> Aubadism [morning-after importunity]
> Aversion
> Condescension
> coping [→Psychology Prima]
> fatalism, material [→Penis Makers and Life
> Destroyers]
> Language Disorders
>> Generative Language Disorder
>> Repetitive Acquisitive Language
>> Disorder
>> [→ Or-Gawp Disease]
> Nariety [a type of neurosis]
>> Nariety of Malapropism

EMOTIONS

personal categories of (-->Categoresis)
philosophical meaning (-->Categoresis)
predictable and unpredictable
        (-->Psychic Prediction)
Psychic Facts
reduction to meaning instead of motivation
        (-->Darwinian Circle)
reliance on old meanings (-->Moral Atavism)
scalar significance (-->Case Studies)
self-sustaining meaning-from-meaning (-->
        Preface)
subjective intentions (-->Literal Delusion)
symbolic (-->Perspective Psychology)
Theory of meaning (-->Emotional Approach to
        Psychology and General Thesis)
ticketed meaning (-->Moral Atavism)
trivial meanings of madness (-->Rhetorical
        Psychology)
ulterior meaning (-->Amalgam)
vs. Oedipus Complex (-->Oedipus Complex)

MEMORY
        And general procedures
                (→ Iterneralism)
        psychic personality and (→Social Personality)
        Memory and Insanity
        Noir Sans
        Psychosomatics
        Realization
        Visionary Aspect

METHODOLOGY (See also Therapy, Psychic)
        Close-Logic of Well-Doing [Mutual Methods]
        Future Psychology
        Inveteration
        Lapsodic Pattern
        Paroxology
        Quadra method -
                Noiac Studies
        Social Stratification Operators
        Universal Psychology

MOODS
  Quasi-functional
    Despotic

MOTIVATION
  literal delusions and (→Literal Delusions)
  positives (→ Positive Ascriptivism)

MIND [See also Conditions, Psyche]
  Apercu
  Improviso
  Objective View of the Mind
  Permiscu

NORMS [See also Tropes]
  As holistic [→Fullrich Effect]
  Combinations vs. individual norms
    [→Paroxology]
  Humor questions [→Comic Sans]
  Laughter
  Literalistic Darwinism
  Marshaled Senses
  Negative Psychology
  Normative disorder [→Rote Disorder]
  Normification
    Of obsession through environment
      [→Intransible Faculty]
  Paradigms in Therapy
  Prodigy as the para-norm [→Prodigy]
  Psychic cloud of [→Voix Faux]
  Psychological norms [→Odd Vote]
  Ungrounded thoughts, and
    [→Mood Kinesthetic]
  Veau Faux

  ABNORMALITY

  Arrested Development as a Function of Four
    Categories

Sexual fetishes as abnormal [→Fullrich Effect]

OBJECTIVITY
Channeling Objectivity
Circumstantial Knowledge
Meaningful Praxis
Objective View of the Mind

OEDIPUS COMPLEX
Oedipus Complex [greed of suspection, orbit
theory]

PARADIGMATIC
Training

PARADOX (See also Irrationalism)
Brain Paradox,
Paradoxical Praxis
Property Paradox

PARANOIA
Ethos of Madness
exponential and relative (→Oedipus Complex)
Metanoia
Noiac Studies
Sacrificial Dilemma
Underworld Theory

PATHOLOGY
Mode Pathology
Negative Psychology
Peduralism
Perspective Pathology
Squirrel Realities
Underworld Theory

PAVLOVIAN
Pavlovian world (→Introduction)
Social Stratification Operators

PERSONALITY (See also Pathology)
    Modes of Approach
    Optimal Personalities
    Social Personality
    Social Psychology [diagram]
    Vertedness
    Zania, The

PERSPECTIVE [See also Psyche, Influences on the Patient and Influences on the Therapist]

    Lack of perspective (→Adequacy)
    Passive / active consequence (→Perspective
        Pathology)
    Passive / active necessity (→Perspective Pa
        Pathology)
    Perspective Psychology
    objective perspectivism [→Positer
        Characteristics]

PITHICS
    Literalistic Darwinism
    New Psychology
    Traditional Psychology

POPULARITY

    Popular Qualifier
    popular sex characteristics [→Property
        Paradox]
    Rorschach test, popularity of [→Art Therapy]

PRACTICE [See also Therapy and Theory]
    Case Studies (using deductive methods)
    Experimental Psychology

PROFESSIONS
    doctors, morticians, soldiers, and comedians
                (→Comic Sans)
    prostitute (*zeit of the 60's*→Contingerion)

PSYCHE
    Metem Psychic [dynamic psyche]
    Negative Psychology
    Perspective Psychology [subjectivity]
    Psyche [background]
    Psychic Facts
    Psychic Prediction
    Psychic Preferences
    Psychic Psychology
    Psychic Techniques

PSYCHIC POWERS
    Psychic Prediction
    Psychic Techniques

PSYCHOLOGISTS [: notes]
    Adler, Adolph [inferiority, lucidity]
    Freud, Sigmund [unconscious and libido]
    Jung, Carl [cognition and symbolism]
    Rank, Otto [unconscious and the future]
    Rogers, Carl [passive therapy]
    Szasz, Thomas [social psychology]

REASON (See also Cognition, Personality, Techniques,
                Therapy)
    New Psychology
    Rational Semantics
    Sanity
    Understanding Genius
    Understanding Intelligence

SUICIDE
>   advice (*avoiding incautious opinions*→
>   Exceptional Psychology)
>   death theme (→Freud, Sigmund)
>   Exceptional Psychology
>   mirth and death (→Penis Makers and Life
>   Destroyers)
>   Self-Harm

SYMBOLS AND ARCHETYPES [Where accompanied by an arrow, see source directed by arrow]

>   Amalgam, The
>   Anima and Animus (→Property Paradox, see
>   also Psyche)
>   Apercu
>   Collective Unconscious
>   crystal, desired (→Social Stratification
>   Operators)
>   Disintegral, The
>   Dream, the (→Collective Unconscious)
>   Elysium (→Collective Unconscious)
>   Encyclopedia (→Collective Unconscious)
>   Extensive Space
>   Fate (→Collective Unconscious)
>   Father Narrative
>   Good and Evil
>   Hero (→Collective Unconscious)
>   Immoral, the (→Collective Unconsious)
>   Improviso, The
>   Innuendo, The
>   Integrator, The
>   Journey (→Collective Unconscious)
>   Language (→Collective Unconscious)
>   Logic (→Collective Unconscious)
>   Miasmos
>   Mystery (→Collective Unconscious)
>   Originalist (→Objective View of the Mind)
>   Parachyrae [lower and higher animals, people]
>   Penis Makers and Life Destroyers
>   Permiscu, The

392

Nathan Coppedge

Nathan Coppedge

BIO

Nathan Coppedge is the author of over 80 books. He has been quoted in Book Forum and the Hartford Courant. He is a member of the International Honor Society for philosophy. A comment at the Economist suggests he may have influenced economic policy in India. Nathan is previously author of articles on psychology at Ezinearticles.com, and is the author of the series of books titled Perpetual Motion Genius Guides, including the Perpetual Motion Genius' Guide for Intelligent Children.